T0146425

Uphill
ONE WAY

*True Stories
from a One-Room
Country School*

RAYMOND L. DYKENS

UPHILL ONE WAY
TRUE STORIES FROM A ONE-ROOM COUNTRY SCHOOL

iUniverse books may be ordered through booksellers or by contacting:

iUniverse
1663 Liberty Drive
Bloomington, IN 47403
www.iuniverse.com
1-800-Authors (1-800-288-4677)

Because of the dynamic nature of the Internet, any web addresses or links contained in this book may have changed since publication and may no longer be valid. The views expressed in this work are solely those of the author and do not necessarily reflect the views of the publisher, and the publisher hereby disclaims any responsibility for them.

Any people depicted in stock imagery provided by Getty Images are models, and such images are being used for illustrative purposes only. Certain stock imagery © Getty Images.

ISBN: 978-1-5320-5063-3 (sc)
ISBN: 978-1-5320-5064-0 (hc)
ISBN: 978-1-5320-5062-6 (e)

Library of Congress Control Number: 2018909171

Print information available on the last page.

iUniverse rev. date: 11/19/2018

In Honor of My Generation

To the many appreciative men and women of my generation who, from the roots of the one-room country school, responded with further education and with a spirit of never giving up. Being difference makers in their respective communities, they have encouraged me to honor them with this writing.

Thank you!

DEDICATION

This book represents a piece of history gone by but not forgotten; a time of not having much while at the same time having everything; and a time to learn, to think, to contribute, and, most importantly, to pass it on. It is in this light that I dedicate this book to my grandchildren. It is presented to have them understand not only what they missed but also what they gained. Dixie, Bode, Sevilla, Eliana, and all children of your generation, may you cherish and respect always your heritage, while at the same time charting new ways, new ideas, and new methods—but always doing so with respect for others and the process of learning. Remember: you have an obligation to pass it on.

As I close this writing, I am happy to report that Dixie Elaine Dykens, age seventeen, is a junior at Lamoni High School in Lamoni, Iowa. Bode Ray Dykens, age fifteen, is a freshman at Lamoni High School in Lamoni, Iowa. Sevilla Dabel Dykens, age eight, is a third grader at the Nettlehorst School in Chicago, Illinois. Eliana Allison Dykens, age five, is in preschool at the Nettlehorst School in Chicago, Illinois. They are all doing wonderfully well in their respective schools, and I will add that the most important aspect of their learning, at this point, is that they all love to read. Secondly, they all are doing their best and having fun in the learning experience. Now, where have I heard these important aspects of learning before? Yep, at good old Scotland Elementary School, back in the day. To all of you I say again that you should do your best, have fun, and pass it on. To my grandchildren I hereby dedicate this book.
     Love, Paw Paw

CONTENTS

PREFACE

You have just read the title of my book and are surely wondering, What? Oh, believe me—I have heard the snickers from many as people like myself have told stories of how it was when they were in school and how they had to walk to school uphill both ways. My story is not like those stories. I tell you the truth. It was, as I have titled my book, uphill one way. You will soon discover that I have given this story the honor of having its own chapter.

This book offers not only the personal experiences of a student educated in a one-room country school but also recollections from my two brothers, Jim and Bob. A typical year would find about thirty students distributed over eight rows of desks. Our school was named after the community of Scotland, an unincorporated community in Jasper County, Missouri, located slightly northwest of the junction of Missouri 66 and Interstate 44. The school sat on the southwest corner of a beautiful prairie. Its picture on the front of this book gives you an idea of its nobility. But unless you could see it change with the seasons, watch jackrabbits run by from its windows, see it full of community members at a box supper, or listen to its environment as students honored it with the process of learning from within its strong and safe structure, you would not be unable to describe it. The town, named after the Reverend Benjamin Scott, has a history that suggests it originated as a small mining district. The time frame of this writing is inclusive of the years 1947 through 1956.

In looking back and reflecting on the community and school of my elementary school days, I can honestly testify to their impact and influence on my life. They were fun, inspiring, and most valuable. Of course, at the time, I had no clue as to how much of an impact they would have on my future. Their value, like many experiences we all have in our lives, grew as I grew. I was a college graduate with a teaching degree in education and about to enter my first employment before I even began to understand the very rich and rewarding education I had received as an elementary student in a one-room country school. As I grew in my experiences as a teacher, a school administrator, and a commander in the US Army National Guard, those Scotland Elementary School days became more and more valuable. It wasn't so much the factual knowledge I relied on as it was the self-discipline, love for reading and writing, ability to get along with others in play and work, ability to utilize the knowledge of those around me to better enhance my own knowledge, accountability for my actions, penchant for always doing my best, and, mostly, the genuine respect I held for not only my teachers but also, and more importantly, my classmates. Of course, at the time, no one said to me, "Ray, remember these principles; they will come in handy one of these days." They were instilled in me by my teacher, parents, community, and fellow classmates. It was a foundation laid for me that allowed me to learn, implement that learning, and make a difference. I am very fortunate to have had this experience.

Finally, after thirty-eight years as a teacher, coach, principal (a role I held for twenty-nine years), and superintendent, during thirty-two years of which I was active in the Missouri National Guard, I can remember saying to myself, "I must record my thoughts and recollections of a time gone by—not just for me but for the heritage and history that will be lost if I don't." I promised myself I would do just that. I am saddened that I did not get it done earlier, but at least at age seventy-five I can share it with those who may have an interest in my thoughts, and I can surely share it with my grandchildren. One day they, too, will look back and perhaps gain an appreciation of where they came from and how important it is that we never forget the lessons taught to us in those precious days as students in the elementary grades. It is my intent that I write in honor of parents, teachers, students, community, and friends. I especially wish to honor my family both then and now.

To place this writing in its proper context, I need to give you a little accounting of the time frame and happenings taking place in not only my history but also the history of America and its focus as I made my entrance into its pulse.

I was born in 1943. This was a time when the mission of every man and woman was to fight, in some way, for our freedoms. The bombing of Pearl Harbor on the seventh day of December 1941 had pulled our nation into war. On June 6, 1944, my father, Charles R. Dykens, landed with the first wave, on Omaha Beach. It was on this same date that General Brehon B. Somervell gave the commencement address to the West Point class of 1944. It is interesting that John Sheldon David Eisenhower, son of Dwight David Eisenhower, the supreme commander of the invasion of Europe, was a member of that graduating class. General Eisenhower was, shall we say, rather busy on that day. But he did send a message to the class. He expressed in this message his full confidence in their "soldierly qualities of devotion to duty, character, and skill." In General Somervell's commencement address, he announced that with the Normandy Invasion, begun a few hours prior to this ceremony, it was now evident that many members of this class would see action in World War II. And, of course, he was correct. They saw action not only in this war but also in Korea, Vietnam, the Middle East, and many other so-called conflicts. Yes, they use real bullets in conflicts. Today the fight continues as we and the whole world fight a world war against terrorist attacks. In his address to West Point graduates, the general went on to say, "How much it will take to achieve victory, no one can predict. Of one fact, and only one, may we be sure. We are going to win!" A roar of applause erupted, and many members of this class and classes to come paid and continue to pay the ultimate sacrifice.

I saw my father when I was three months of age and did not see him again until I was nearly three years of age. My mother, Muriel E. Palmer Dykens, was my preschool teacher. No, she was not a certified teacher. She, like most parents in those days, was expected to prepare her children for their entry into the public school setting. Preschools, at least public preschools, had not yet been established. For that matter, kindergarten was almost nonexistent.

The argument in those days was "Do I start my child in grade one at the age of five or wait until the age of six?" While I never had a vote, I am glad I started at age six. As a professional educator, I learned that most boys mature later than most girls. Not only do they mature later than girls physically, but they also develop a readiness to learn later. While this same conclusion still holds true today, I have come to agree that preschool and kindergarten are great opportunities for *all* children to learn, if given the appropriate condition of each and every one's readiness to learn.

Because of my parents, I was ready to enter the first grade at Scotland Elementary School in 1948. I am very thankful for the opportunities the one-room schoolhouse afforded me. And while it couldn't compete with the opportunities afforded our youth today, it instilled in me some values that have sustained me and allowed me many opportunities to succeed. It was a time in history when our country was truly tested. I have no doubt that because of soldiers like Master Sergeant Charles R. Dykens and the sacrifices they made, we are today a free nation. To all who serve at home and abroad, I say *thank you*! This is a book of true stories from the one-room country school and the community that supported it. It's about learning, working, discipline, doing your best, having fun, and treating others the way you wish to be treated. I sincerely hope that you find in my stories some insight of a lost and nearly forgotten time in our history as a nation. Who knows—you may even have a laugh or two. I hope so! That is what I remember most about our school: we had fun! Learning was fun! Playing was fun! And yes, graduation was fun! Graduation was an honor, and for me a time of reflection as I let my mind take me back through the experiences of my one-room country school days.

"There is no way he did that," you may say. Yes, I did graduate, and no, I probably didn't think too much about my experiences on that evening. Today, though, as I begin this book, it really is as if I am seated on that stage on that graduation night in 1956. I can, indeed, look back and remember so many wonderful—and some not-so-wonderful—experiences. Regardless, they were all learning experiences. And so, before I get to the part where we accept our diplomas and take off on an eighth-grade graduation trip, I shall share some of those experiences with you. The ones I share are all true, at least to the best of my recollection. Some are funny, some sad, and I am confident they will spur memories for those of my generation. For the rest of you, my hope is that they will be an entertaining history lesson. This was a time in our history that perhaps didn't hold as many opportunities as we see in today's world, and yet it was a time that prepared us to take a step forward and beyond what our grandparents and even our parents had the opportunity to do. I am not saying I received a great education. I am saying we learned a whole lot more than the three Rs, and I can honestly say that in today's society, perhaps we should get back to some of the ideals taught to us in the one-room country school. I have some real thoughts on some of this, and perhaps one day I will express them, but for now I want to share with you the ups and downs of my one-room country school.

I am well aware my book will not be a best seller. It doesn't have all the ingredients that many folks like to read in today's literature. Couple that with the fact that it is not well written and lacks a good writing style, and you have yourself a book that is real, honest, nostalgic, mostly true, and probably boring to most. But it is my story, and I'm sticking to it. My only motive is a genuine desire to pass it along to my family. Some of you may not be familiar with the world as I saw it during this period in the history of our nation. It was a determination of recovery from an awful world war. And this recovery was not just economic but perhaps even more so a time of healing our wounds, both physical and mental.

Just to give you an idea of the time frame in which these stories take place, I will include early in Chapter 1, a picture taken in 1949. My dad was finally home from WWII, I had a little brother named Jimmy, and I was now enrolled in Scotland Elementary School. Our family went on to raise three boys. I was five years older than Jim, and our brother, Bob, came along when I was nine. As you will see from this book, we all were proud of our Scotland Elementary School experience.

I will begin my book with an opening chapter that will mention my first home with both my mom and my dad and our first move as a family to what would become my new home. I was about to enter the wonderful experiences of the one-room country school. As you imagine the setting and picture the wide eyes I had, the dreams I was starting to live, and the good times ahead of me, I truly hope you will read my book and let yourself not only visualize that time but also, more importantly, better appreciate the opportunities afforded you in today's world. It is my desire that the value of the one-room country school and the impact it had on our great nation never be forgotten. It indeed was a foundational cornerstone of America.

ACKNOWLEDGMENTS

I would like to express special thanks to all who provided pictures, stories, and general information about the days of the one-room country schoolhouse.

To Glenna, my wife of fifty-five years and counting, who is also a product of a one-room country schoolhouse. You have been my best teacher.

To Alan, Amy, Andy and Lauren, our sons and daughters in law, for their encouragement and persistence that I write this stuff down.

To my grandchildren, Dixie, Bode, Sevilla, and Elliana, for posing for pictures and for giving me the motivation to give this a try.

To Jim and Bob, my brothers. They both had experiences from this same little school, and they both passed their learning on to others as teachers.

To my teachers. I have been so blessed to have received the very best teachers at all levels of my learning experiences.

To all Scotland Elementary School alumni. You are a large part of making my experience a most beautiful one.

To the Scotland community in total. It was truly a village that raised children and worked together to get it done.

To my parents, Charles and Muriel Dykens, who taught me to work hard, do my best, and respect others.

And, finally, to others whose names may or may not be specifically mentioned in the book but who contributed testimonies of this same one-room schoolhouse experience with their stories, pictures, and encouragement. I will list a few players who made up the school and community and helped me have the experiences that I cherish. I'll list them as they come to mind, and yes, I will forget to mention some. Please forgive me. My doctor tells me I have "old timer's." I have to leave my house at least three times before I can finally go. I have my keys, wallet, phone, list … and now where is it I am going? Some of you understand, don't you?

I am remembering some last names of families who were my neighbors and supporters of the Scotland community and its school. A few of them had more than one family in the Scotland community proper. To list them would only mean that I may forget someone, and that would not be my intent. Just know that if you, like me, remember our days together, please also know that I benefited from your presence and that I cherish my days and years spent in Scotland, Missouri.

It is an old saying, but in the case of the Scotland community and Scotland Elementary School, it truly did necessitate this village, at least during the time frame of the forties, fifties, and even the sixties, coming together, working together, sharing together, and playing together so that all kids growing up in that neighborhood could have opportunities to grow not only physically but mentally as well. I can't help but wonder if maybe we need to rekindle that spirit somewhat in this great nation. That is just a thought for perhaps another writing or at least some discussion.

OUR FIRST MOVE

In the past seventy-five years, I have moved many times. I can think of at least twenty-three moves. I've written them down someplace, but I don't remember where. The number of moves isn't important. What I do remember is that each move was an exciting adventure and taught me many lessons of life. Perhaps the greatest lesson I have learned from all these moves is what my parents taught me while never saying a word. If they had put it into words, they would have said, "Remember that home is where you are." Another valuable lesson I learned is that each geographic area is different both in features and in the habits of its inhabitants. This doesn't mean the inhabitants are right or wrong; more importantly, it means that their valued opinions should at least be respected. This helped me a bunch in my work. For example, when I would begin a new job in a new location, I was always careful to not make too many changes too soon. I learned to sell needed change while respecting what was already in place. Sometimes I learned that change wasn't necessary. Please don't misunderstand; I am not suggesting you should move often, but that was the way my life turned out. My family, which now included a baby brother, left our home at 1730 Missouri in Joplin, Missouri, for a new home in Scotland, Missouri.

I'll leave most of my Scotland experiences for later chapters, but I do want you to know that it was a move that put an exclamation point on the first five years of my life. I guess you could call those my preschool years. I was leaving my familiar surroundings and getting ready to start my go-to-school life. I know, as I look back, that this was the main reason for our move. My parents wanted me to go to a small rural school. They had both been raised in a country setting, and while Dad was employed in Joplin as a mechanic at Reno Motor Company, and even though they had friends in Joplin and lived in a fine community, they decided it was the best thing to do for the education of their children. It wasn't that Joplin did not have fine schools. In fact, they had and still have very good schools. Those schools were just too big to suit my parents. I can tell you that my parents did stay in contact with their Joplin friends over the years and continued to treasure their friendships.

I can remember being excited about our new home. I use the term "new home" when perhaps I should be using "different home." I was about to move into a very big house with a big yard, and I would be near other kids my age. And yes, it really was a huge house and a huge yard. The house was made of rocks. It had two stories, with the upstairs not yet finished and the downstairs needing some more remodeling. The yard was, as I remember it, way too big to rake. But that would soon become one of my jobs. My dad worked very hard over the years to fix this house up. It was for me a most wonderful time of my life. I had pets, friends, and my own room, and to top it off we eventually had an indoor bathroom. It took several years to get running water into the house and to get a bathroom, but we got it done. I say "we" because that is the truth. My dad was the engineer, but, believe me—I did help. It not only took a lot of work; it also took money—money we didn't have. But with some basic sacrifices, we saved it. I realize I am getting ahead of myself as I try to portray the first five preschool years of my life. I salute my parents, who made sure those five years were a positive learning experience for me and my brothers-to-be.

I will go ahead and mention that during my very first year in the Scotland community, I had a swing with a tire tied to the end of it. I also had a cow that had to have water carried to her. Dad soon found some land and a barn to rent. Our herd, over my grade school years, grew from one cow to at least five milk cows and a steer or two. Yes, I learned to milk cows, doctor calves, and fix fence. And yes, the big yard still had to be raked. So I was learning not only how to play but also how to work. And, most importantly, I was happy.

AUTHOR'S HOME, BIKE, Swing

No, I never forgot 1730 Missouri. Even today, in 2018, I still have the opportunity to drive by and see the first home I had after Dad returned from the war. The house is gone, the garage that I carried wood from is gone, and I don't recognize any of the neighbors.

Yes, we heated with a wood-burning stove located in the living room. There was also a stove in the kitchen that Mom needed wood for to cook our meals. Between the two stoves, we kept from freezing in the winter. Speaking of freezing, we never had a freezer. What we did have was an icebox. Yep, the iceman brought us a big block of ice on a regular basis, and that kept our food refrigerated—well, most of the time. I am not telling you this to complain. I remember my parents both commenting on how fortunate they were to have a good cookstove and a good source of heat. Anyway, the lot is exactly the same. It looks small now, but then it was huge. Why is that?

Yes, my first home was a good one—not because of the structure, necessarily; the location; the garage, sandbox, friends, or the movie theater on Main Street; or the size. It was good because my parents worked really hard at making it more than just a place to live. It was home—my first home, and one filled with good memories. Well, there were a few memories I would just as soon forget though they still linger—memories like a serious wasp sting I got when I stepped off the back porch barefoot, lying in bed with the mumps, losing my big toenail under the front gate, having my scooter stolen off my front porch, and so on. On the other hand, I remember a baby brother coming home from the hospital and me being disappointed that he couldn't even play with me, and my grandfather Dykens visiting me all the way from Smith Center, Kansas, which at that time was not an easy thing to do. I'll never forget the old man who lived down the block and was my best friend having my picture taken while I was on a pony—an experience that would cause me to fall in love with horses. These all became precious memories in my life. Yes, I am thankful for my preschool home and its teachings. Now it is time to move on to my next "actually going to a school" years.

The following pictures are of the pony I had my picture taken on at 1730 Missouri. It was my first experience of being on a horse, and I've loved them ever since. The next picture is a reminder to me of how many times I carried in wood from this garage. The third picture is a memory for me of the time I stepped on a wasp as I stepped off the back porch barefoot. And the last one is a picture of my grandfather Dykens in front of our home. I never got to spend much time with him, and so, again, it is a precious memory.

RAY DYKENS 1947

JOPLIN GRANDPA DYKENS 1946

These are my beginnings of getting ready to go to school, and we all have them. I share mine as a reminder that time goes by so quickly, and so I challenge you each to build those precious memories and use them for sustainment as you go through life.

There really is no chronology to this writing in terms of first year, second year, and so forth. I write as a thought pops into my head. This is a story that is lengthy and will span some happenings and experiences both good and not so good. They happened at or near a one-room country school named Scotland Elementary School—a community school located in Jasper County, Missouri. It lies about four miles east of Duenweg and eight miles east of Joplin, Missouri. The closet place of employment was, at that time, Atlas Powder Company. Atlas had its own school and was a community between Duenweg and Scotland and perhaps a few miles north. Today Scotland School is identified on maps as a location lying next to Interstate 44. It served not only the children of the community of Scotland but also other children that lived within the district boundaries. Even though many of these students didn't live in the Scotland community, we still considered them community members. Anyway, I wish at this time, before getting into my actual school life, to share with you some stories about my experiences in the community itself. I do this because many of my experiences were so intertwined between the community and the school that they became one and the same. I'll try to not repeat stories, but my grandkids and my own kids tell me I am not very good at that. So like I tell them, "Get over it and listen." My only fear is that I might not tell them the same way, since this is a book of true stories. We'll see. I will start with a story of one of my many pets, Ole Corky, and go from there.

Pets were always a big part of my life. The stories of my pets include both happy and sad experiences. Most of you know what I am speaking of. But they taught me so much. They were a very important part of my preschool learning. I have a concern that in our world of today, many children do not have the opportunity to learn from animals. What a shame. They have much to teach us.

Our dog Corky was one of my very favorite teachers. I don't remember exactly when we got Corky. I know he grew up with me at Scotland. He etched his memory into my brain as a result of many happenings. But the one I remember most was his ride on the running board of our car. Every Saturday, we would make a trip to Joplin to get our groceries for the week ahead. It was a grocery store on Second Street, just east of Main. I don't remember the name of the store, but I do remember the owners were very good to my folks and often gave them credit if they were short on cash for that week.

Anyway, Ole Corky was a "for sure" member of our family. He was a border collie and was very smart. On one of our Saturday trips to Joplin, as we drove down Main Street, I was hoping we might get to go to a movie. We didn't get to go to the movies often, but once in a while we were rewarded with this experience. People kept pointing at us and looking down at our car on the passenger side. Dad figured that maybe we had a low tire or maybe something was hanging out of a door. So he pulled over to check it out. There on the running board was our dog Corky.

Most cars today don't have running boards. But in those days, they all did. It was an important step that allowed entrance into the big car. As I recall, it was about ten to twelve inches wide. Now, mind you, we had driven all the way into Joplin from Scotland—a distance of about eight miles—on a busy highway at whatever the speed limit was. I would guess it to be at least fifty miles per hour. We had made several sharp turns, stopped and started several times, and even passed a couple of cars. Dad was pretty good at passing other cars. Anyway, there Corky was, his claws dug into the running board, and he actually seemed to be enjoying the ride.

The adults could not understand how in the world he survived that ride. I was too young to worry about that; I just knew he would be better off in the car, riding with me. Of course, that happened. And no, we never took him to Joplin again—at least not to our knowledge. We did check the running boards often, and after giving it some more thought, I am betting Ole Corky decided he had made a very poor decision and thus opted not to try that again.

Old Corky lived to be an old dog and survived other near-fatal accidents. I saw him chase cars and bite their wheels several times. The result each time, of course, would be that he would fly through the air and take quite a tumble. I don't know if the two stories are related, but it appeared to me that he just did not like cars. My brothers, Jim and Bob, also enjoyed Ole Corky. He was a very good teacher of what not do to. And he was one of our very best friends.

I know my book is about a one-room country school, but it would be an injustice not to mention the number of dogs that followed their kids to school, some of which even waited for them until school was out. They were a part of our school. I'll title this story "Saving My Dog." This story is one that parents could use to explain to their children that no matter how much you love your pets, you should not go into the street to save them. The dog in this case was a small but feisty dog of some kind. I'll call him a mixed breed. I had just moved to Scotland and was barely the age of five. He was a pet that preceded Ole Corky by two or three years. I am ashamed that I can't remember his name, but I remember calling him Blacky. Perhaps that was his name. Regardless, I knew he was mine and that he taught me a great lesson. Looking back on it, it was a lesson I used many times as I attended the one-room country school. I have two short stories about this little black dog.

The first one is about one of the lessons he taught me. I was at the neighborhood store, which was located on a busy highway that went into Joplin. This would have been at least three blocks from my home. Should I have been down there alone? Of course not. Scotland's only store at the time was located at this junction. It was sort of a general store. I had found some pennies and decided I would go shopping. The store was on my side of the highway, and so I did not have to cross the road to get there. The store sat on a slope, and the highway followed the same slope, so cars would come over the slope and be right in front of the store before they knew it. My mom, of course, had no idea I had ventured out on my own.

Anyway, there I was. All of a sudden, my dog let out a big yelp. As I looked up, I saw him in the middle of the highway. He was on the slope, and he had been hit by a car. I immediately ran to him and crouched over him, not knowing what to do. I can remember some cars swerving and going around me. I remember standing in the middle of that road, holding my dog in my arms, and the owners of the store rushing to my side and helping me and my dog get to safety. I don't know for sure how close a call I experienced on that day. I do know that as I listened to others talk about it, they had all been afraid for my life. I could, even at that young age, remember feeling that I was glad I was not hurt and how grateful my mom was that I was okay.

I carried my dog, with my mom's help, all the way back to our house. The dog was very badly injured. I know there was talk of putting him down, but my mom said she would do what she could to save him. She did, and we did save him. He recovered but was never the same. Yet we still had fun together, and for the next couple of years before his passing, I was grateful for his friendship and loyalty.

Again, I am thankful for the lessons I learned from that experience. Firstly, I learned that the highway is a dangerous place. It was then, and it most certainly is now. In the next eight years of my walking to school and crossing that same highway many, many times, I was always very careful. No one needed to remind me ever again. I had learned the dangers of traffic on a highway the hard way. Secondly, this little dog taught me that love can cure. My mom never gave me false hope; she said only that she would try. With all of us trying our best, it worked out.

Other stories about Scotland were sprinkled into my preschool years and into my upbringing. They were all testimonies of a community raising kids together. I suspect—in fact, I know— that I did my share to keep them all busy. Perhaps one or two more stories will surface as I plunge into my years at Scotland Elementary School. As far as I am concerned, the bottom line is this: God put pets here for a reason. Mine have all helped me on my journey through life. I've had many pets, and I have enjoyed them all. Even at age seventy-five, my wife and I have two rescued black-and-white dogs, and yes they are a chore, but we love Mabel and Molly.

They, too, have an interesting story, but I will save that for another writing perhaps. I hope the readers of my stories have enjoyed learning from their pets as well. They are indeed a blessing.

Playing in the snow, just as it is now, was a fun, fun deal. That is one thing that has not changed much over the years. My grandchildren would rather play in the snow than eat. Well, that may be a stretch, and since this is all about telling the truth, I will at least say it is one of those pleasures that past generations and future generations enjoyed and will continue to enjoy. Please tell me that is a fact. Sometimes I do worry about our country taking care of its environment and ensuring its beauty for years to come.

CHAPTER 2

A NEW BEGINNING (EIGHTH-GRADE GRADUATION)

There we were, my whole eighth-grade class, waiting to march in through the back door of our one-room country school. All three of us were graduating, and we all felt we had earned it together. Looking back on it, I now know we all had different talents, and each of us contributed to the final result of getting to march into the school together for our eighth-grade graduation. Our path to the front was outlined for us to proceed down the aisle, between the fourth- and fifth-grade rows of seats, and take our place on the graduation stage. Mary Kendrick, Janice Trenton, and I were proud and eager to participate in this commencement exercise. This was our night. We had passed the eighth-grade comprehensive examination and had officially been approved by both our teacher and the county superintendent to graduate from the eighth grade at the Scotland Elementary School in District 118. We marched in as "Pomp and Circumstance" was being played thanks to a 78 rpm record player. As we approached the stage area, we passed through a short white fence that had been erected all the way across the front of the stage. There were five chairs set in place: Three for the graduates, one for our guest speaker, and one for our teacher.

We stood proudly in front of the middle three chairs with our speaker to the right of us and our teacher to the left. The music stopped, and I removed my cap while a prayer was offered, followed by the Pledge of Allegiance. Since I was honored as the valedictorian, it had been my privilege to choose our speaker. I had chosen Herman Plumb, the pastor of the church I attended in Carthage, Missouri. I guess I figured that perhaps we needed a little guidance from above.

Following the pledge, we took our seats. The events become a little vague at this point. I would blame all the years that have gone by, but the truth is that we were graduating and that was all I had on my mind. I do remember our teacher had some very meaningful and complimentary remarks, and our guest speaker had some sound advice to give. I do remember being proud of him and being thankful that his speech was short, entertaining, and powerful. It was powerful because he talked about how powerful an impact we could make in our lives if we did our best and invited God to walk with us on our journey.

Needless to say, this was a special night. It was more of a big deal back then to actually graduate from the eighth grade than it is these days. Don't get me wrong; it is still a big deal today to graduate, and it should be. But for us it wasn't so much of an expectation as it was an accomplishment to better prepare us for the next step. We recognized the importance of a good education, and even though we were only eighth graders, we knew it was, indeed, an important accomplishment. I would be remiss if I didn't say that we were a little scared. We all had plans to go on to high school, and we all knew things would be different there. We would be going from one room to many rooms, from one teacher to many teachers, from a lot of individual help to a lot of responsibility in applying a lot more time to the books and in competing at the next level. We honestly felt we could because our teacher assured us of that happening. Still, the apprehension was real. But on this night, we put those future goals, dreams, and fears on the back burner. This was our night to be proud and to celebrate.

We were proud to be there in our blue caps and gowns. This was in keeping with our class color of blue. And yes, we did have class rings. I still have mine. It is with my graduation speech, I think. We also had a class song. I am not sure how we came about choosing it, unless it perhaps was one that someone could play

15

on the piano and that we could all sing. Its title was "I Would Be True." A few of you reading this will recognize it, but most of you, I suspect, will need to do some research. The three of us sang it that night, and I swear to you it brought tears to my eyes. Some might have said I had tears because it was not well prepared or perhaps because I was sad. Not so! I really was caught up in the moment. I still tear up often, and you know what? That's okay.

3

UPHILL ONE WAY (TO AND FROM SCHOOL)

Getting to school and getting back was an educational experience in itself. Thus it has its own separate title and dedicated space in my book. The distance from my house to the schoolhouse was 1.8 miles if one stuck to the roadways. There were several shortcuts available, but trust me; they took longer. According to my research on the Scotland community and its elevation on a topographic map, the elevation of my house was about 1,033 feet. The elevation of the school was about 1,057 feet. That is a difference of twenty-four feet. Yep, it was uphill all right. Remember: I learned basic math skills in a one-room country school, and I feel I did okay. But if you wish, you may research this yourself. Either way, and even if you disagree, I am sticking to my *true* story that, in my opinion, it was uphill one way.

It is true that we did walk a good deal of the time. There was sort of a car pool that functioned if conditions permitted. Its use was primarily restricted for times of inclement weather or for special occasions when someone was going that way anyhow. Even when the car pool was scheduled to run, it had its setbacks. Many of these failures were simply due to failure of the car to start. Or perhaps the priorities had changed and the car had to be used for something more important, like getting to work. Often the car was just plain old out of gas and it was not yet pay day. My dad's employer was in Joplin, Missouri. Joplin was about eight miles away. He was always aware of those times when his car was to be the designated car for the transportation of students to Scotland School. He tried his best during those days to find other ways to get to his place of work so as not to tie up the car. Reno Motor Company in Joplin was his place of employment, and they were good to him and did their best to work with him and be as flexible as possible to help out. They were glad to do that because he was their best mechanic and they didn't want to lose him. That's no brag, just a fact.

Anyway, when transportation was not possible, we walked. It isn't that I wouldn't want my grandkids to have this same experience, but in this day and age, it simply would not be a safe thing to do. Adult supervision has become a full-time necessity. That's too bad! For me and my classmates, going to school was more of a "We'll have to hurry, or we'll be late" mission. Believe it or not, we were seldom late. That is, in getting there we were seldom late. Now, getting home from school was a different matter. We did have a tendency to play along the way. One of our very favorite things to do was to stop and have some possum grapes. There was a huge tree before we got to the main highway (Route 166), and this tree was loaded with vines full of globs of juicy possum grapes. I climbed up in that tree many times just to sit on a limb, eat grapes, and dream of being a big-league baseball player someday.

Side note: At age five, my parents took me to my first professional baseball game. We went to Saint Louis to see the Cardinals play the Dodgers. Stan Musial, Marty Marion, Del Rice, and Enos Slaughter are names that come to mind. Yep, I and all my family are Cardinals fans. It isn't an option. As I write this story in 2018, I confess it took some intestinal fortitude to remain loyal to my Cards, but I did.

Back to my story. Once in a while, we would cut through the woods and hunt some turtles so we could have some turtle races. When we were not able to find turtles, we would chase each other through the trees, trying to lose one another. Regardless of our chosen route home, at least for those of us that actually lived in the Scotland community, we had to cross a creek. Most of the year it was dry, but during heavy rains it flowed deep and wide. During these times, it sported some very swift currents that flowed over a very rocky bottom. The rule given us by our parents was not to use the highway bridge unless water was flowing in the creek. And if we did use the bridge, we were to hurry across, being sure no cars were in sight. This was Route 166 and today is known as Seventh Street in Joplin. It is very near the famous Route 66, and even in the '40s and '50s it was a very busy highway. The bridge was narrow, so hurrying across was a very good rule. Of course, there were times when our interpretation of the creek running too high was not the same as our parents'. Wet clothes were easily explained as an accidental fall and landing in a shallow pool of water. I am sure our excuses were received in complete confidence as the gospel truth.

I wouldn't trade these walks for anything. Yep, it was cold in the winter and hot in the summer. And yes, we were kids who took chances we shouldn't have. (Don't kid yourself.) The chances we took and choices we made were far safer than the choices our children and grandchildren have to make today. We teased each other, fought some, played too much, and got sick on possum grapes and green apples more than once. I was a slow learner. Don't misunderstand my confession; I'm not talking about bullying as we know it in today's society. On the contrary, we took care of each other. We watched out for the little ones, and we held hands at the creek and at all road crossings. And guess what—we talked! We didn't hurry home to the TV or video games. Not that we wouldn't have, had we had them.

We grew in these walks as we breathed in fresh air. Actually, Atlas Powder Company was only about three miles away, and so I may not be accurate when I proclaim the air was fresh. We talked, laughed, ran, jumped, and even cried some. We discovered many good and bad things along the way. We learned what to avoid, such as poison ivy, certain snakes, and skunks. And we learned what a pleasure it was for our moms when we presented them with a beautiful flower we had picked along the way. (This was especially beneficial when we were late or our pants were wet from falling in the creek.)

I understand that hearing these stories is boring to the young people of today. I know they don't want to hear about the good old days. And I am equally confident that they do not want to hear about walking uphill to school. But for my grandchildren, this isn't an option. By golly, they are going to hear them. It's their heritage, and I truly believe they can learn lessons from them that can be applied to the experiences they are having today. I guess one could say, "Poor me; I had to walk to school." But truly, I loved it! Truly, I benefited from it! And truly, I wish my children and grandchildren could have that same experience! Sorry, kids; this is how I truly feel. Of course, in today's world, this would not be safe or even practical. I understand that, and I challenge you to record your experiences for future reference so that all children of your generation can reflect back someday and say, "I am proud of where I came from."

I cannot leave this train of thought pertaining to my travel to and from school without sharing with you a story of perhaps my most prized school journey. It involves our horse. I say "our horse" because it was shared by not only my brothers but also by the entire community of Scotland. This is one other method of transportation to school I have not yet mentioned. Yes, I had a horse, so why didn't I ride her to school? There are lots of reasons for this that I won't go into, most of which were good reasons. But on one occasion, I did get to ride my horse to school.

This picture gives you a glimpse of one of my very best friends, Ole Queen.

Before I get to the story of taking my horse to school, I must tell you about this wonderful horse, Ole Queen. She was special, and these comments will better help you to understand the role she played on the day I was to take her to Scotland Elementary School. First, you should realize that my pets were a part of my preschool experience and education, and they continued to be all through my schooling. Mom and Dad worked with me on numbers, letters, following rules, work ethic, and listening skills, but much of my preschool learning took place in my backyard. There I made up games with friends, and my mom often filled in. One of our favorite games with her was to pretend I was Roy Rogers and she was Dale Evans. Some of you know who these folks are. Others may have to research. More than once I stood at my mom's side while she was working in the kitchen and said, "I am going out to the north forty and check on the cows." She would reply, "Roy, you be careful, and you be back in time for dinner, you hear?" Off I would gallop on my pretend horse, Trigger. And that brings me to my story of our horse, Ole Queen. It is a true story, as all my stories are. And since Ole Queen was very influential in my schooling, I will share with you about this beautiful animal and even include her part in being sure the students at Scotland School and its community all got rides.

Ole Queen was a kids' horse for sure. What a horse! While that is a true statement, I admit I did not know what a good horse was at age nine or ten. I am not sure how old I was when we got Queen. But my brother Jim was up and going strong, and so I suspect I was about ten. I remember wanting a horse so much. I was into playing cowboy, and besides, I needed some transportation. I've learned since that there are horses and then there are *horses*. My dad knew horses. He had participated in rodeos when he was a young man and had grown up in an environment where horses were a way of life. So while he wanted me to have a horse, he wanted to be sure it was a horse that was kid friendly.

Of course, money was an issue. After all, this would be for pleasure. It wasn't a work horse or a needed head of stock in any way. It was for fun. My dad was in favor of fun, but at the same time, the needs of the family came first. I am very positive it was a major sacrifice for my parents to make this purchase. But I could sense it was in the air and that the possibilities were growing stronger. There was much talk at the table about safety, rules, responsibility, care, and the like. Yes, this was a time when families sat together at a table and talked. By the way, I am proud to say that both of our boys, Alan and Andy, and their families still do this.

Somewhere along the line, Dad hinted that a horse may be too expensive and that perhaps a donkey would do. I remember trying to be brave and even agreeing that if we couldn't have a horse, a donkey would be okay. But I didn't mean it. And of course, my parents knew I was fibbing. In a way, it made them proud. All you parents out there know what I mean. Anyway, a horse was in my dreams. It was a beautiful day when a trailer pulled up in front of our house. Yep, I knew the trailer was stopping at our house to unload. My dad was quick to remind me that horses were expensive and that he didn't want me to be disappointed. Again, I was brave. I knew then that my parents had purchased a donkey and that although it wasn't a horse, it would be mine. As the tailgate was lowered, I tried to show them I was happy. I could see the tail end of what I believed was a huge donkey. It was black and big. I was excited and could not wait to see the rest of this animal.

Out she backed, very gently—proud, big, and beautiful. I don't know for sure when it hit me, but I think it was not until the animal was fully unloaded and standing tall in front of me. "That is no donkey. It's a horse; it's a horse!" I screamed it over and over again and again at the top of my lugs. "It's a horse!"

I am sure that as you read this, you too can remember some precious moments in your life that gave you these same kinds of feelings, so I won't try to explain them. Of course, I was one excited young man. But I have come to a realization over the years of the feelings my parents must have experienced on this occasion. Because of my being a parent and a grandparent, I've had these same feelings. There is no greater excitement in the world than seeing the happiness in the eyes of your children when a dream comes true. So did I go on during the next several years to have a great time with Ole Queen? You bet! But it was not nearly as good a time as I have had over the years enjoying and continuing to enjoy my family. Wow! What a blessing.

Yes, Ole Queen went on to make her mark. Every kid in the Scotland community learned to ride on Ole Queen. She was indeed a kids' horse. She loved kids, and she protected them. Falling off a horse is a part of learning to ride a horse. It usually isn't the horse's fault. It just happens. Did I and others fall off of Ole Queen? Yep, many times. And every time, she would stop dead still so as not to step on us, nudge us with her nose as if to see if we were okay, and then wait patiently while we figured out a way to climb back on. A horse that won't stop when its rider falls is, in my opinion, not a good horse. Queen was a very good horse.

Now, getting back on to ride again was a challenge. For a long time, we didn't have a saddle. We couldn't afford one. When we did fall off or get on for our first ride of the day, we would lead Queen over to a stump or maybe a chair we had sitting in the yard, or anything handy that would allow us to climb on. She just stood there and waited. Amazing! I saw as many as four kids on her at one time. This was not advisable, but it didn't matter to her.

Her name was Queen. I don't know for sure where that name came from, but it sounds original enough to have come from me. Ole Queen went on to be our horse for years. In fact, I and both my brothers rode her during our high school years. The farmer guy came out more and more in my dad during these days. He was raised in a family of farmers in Smith Center, Kansas. He loved cattle and all that went with them. Anyway, by now we had accumulated a small herd of cattle and had them located on some rented land with a barn about a quarter mile from our house. My learning to work and accept responsibility for myself as well as my brothers increased rapidly. I remember one particular incident that happened as I had mounted Queen to go check on the cattle before I headed to one of my high school basketball games. I finally found them in a far-off back pasture and was running Ole Queen pretty hard as I headed back to the barn. She was hard to hold back once she knew she was headed to the barn. Then it happened. She stepped in a hole, stumbled, and fell. I hit the ground out in front of her. I remember feeling her roll over me. In fact, I felt her get about halfway over and then kick to roll fully over. As this happened, I was right in the middle of the small of her back, facedown in the mud. Thank God the ground was soft. She made it over, I led her on to the barn, and we were both okay. I was hurting with some bruised ribs, but nothing was broken.

I went to the game but couldn't play that night, as I was in some pain. No matter; I was only averaging about four or five points a game. If you are a kid reading this, I am just kidding. What matters isn't how many points you score; it is how hard you try and that you do your best. It is true, though, that 4.5 points was my average, but I did play very good defense and was an okay passer.

To this day, I honestly feel my life was saved because I was riding bareback. Had she rolled over me with the saddle on, I would have been in some big-time trouble. I have many, many Queen stories, but you get the idea. I loved that horse, and she loved me.

I am not saying she was perfect. In her later years, when I was a pretty good rider, she would try to get me off her back by running under a tree with a low limb. I never faulted her for that. She was ready to retire, but I wouldn't let her.

But finally she did retire. She went to live at the home of my uncle Morris. He lived near Wentworth, Missouri. Actually he lived very close to a one-room country school named Dry Valley. Anyway, he had a farm and some kids that needed a horse to ride— one that was gentle and one they could learn on. Yep, Ole Queen retired to a life of once again helping kids learn to ride safely. She was quite a horse. Once she was able to let little kids ride her again instead of me, she didn't use the tree trick to get them off. At least, I never heard of it happening. Not long after that, she was put out to pasture on the small farm of my grandparents, Etta and William Palmer. Their son, my uncle Jack, a lover of all animals and a grown man at this point, took care of Ole Queen and provided for her care until her death. She had a good and long life and was properly buried on my grandparents' farm. I still visited her once in a while. She knew me and was always glad to see me. Ole Queen touched lots of lives—not just those of kids but those of all of us. We all learned from her, and we all loved her; and most importantly, she loved us back. I was lucky to have her in my life.

HAPPY TRAILS: MY HORSE RIDE TO AND FROM SCHOOL

Now that you are better aquatinted with Ole Queen, I will get back to my story of my ride to Scotland School. She was one of a kind, so you now perhaps understand better why my parents trusted me to have this experience. The words "Happy trails" are from a Dale Evans song used as the theme song of *The Roy Rogers Show*. "Happy trails to you, until we meet again." I wanted so much to ride Ole Queen, my horse, to school. But for all the right reasons, the answer from my parents continued to be no. However, late in my eighth-grade year, persistence paid off—or maybe it was because I had won the trust of my parents and proven that I was a responsible person. I'm going with that. As I recall, I and my brother Jim climbed aboard one early morning and headed for the school. My other brother, Bob, had not yet started school. My instructions were clear, and there was no doubt in my mind as to who was responsible for this journey. It was I. And that was okay with me. I was proud! My instructions from my parents were as follows:

1. Stay on the path we have agreed on, and don't run the horse.
2. Upon arrival, tie her to a shade tree and bring her a bucket of water. Keep it full.
3. With the teacher's permission, you may give rides. You will walk and lead the horse.
4. Older kids who know how to ride may do so only if they ride double with you.
5. Pull some green grass, and be sure she has all she wants.
6. Come directly home. No possum grapes. No side trips. No turtle hunts. Walk the horse.
7. She will want to run as soon as she catches sight of the barn. Don't let her!

If you are reading this story and thinking, *What were his parents thinking?* or *It's a good thing Child Protective Services were not yet available to call*, please don't. My parents were great and would never have put me or my brothers in harm's way. You have to first of all understand that every kid in Scotland had already ridden Queen. She truly was a kids' horse. She loved kids. The only concern my parents had was that Queen always did exactly what we commanded her to do. So it was on me to do the right thing. Secondly, I am sure there was a genuine concern for the welfare of the horse, as she would have to stand tied to a tree all day. But they made the decision that I, as an eighth grader, could surely handle this responsibility.

And handle it I did. In fact, I took it a little too seriously. I worked really, really hard that day. I worried about my brother, my friends, my horse, and even my mom. I carried water, I pulled grass, I supervised rides while everyone else was playing, and I didn't once let Queen run, even though she wanted to. That wasn't easy, because when I rode her, I always let her have a good run, and she knew that. Yes, I learned a lot about responsibility that day. I learned a lot about trust. I learned a lot about sacrifice. I learned a lot about sharing. I even learned what it feels like to do a job and do it well. I would say my parents knew exactly what they were doing.

Wouldn't you? I never rode Ole Queen to school again, as this took place in the spring of my eighth-grade year and school at Scotland would be letting out in the middle of April. I have never forgotten that special day and what it meant to me. For my parents to trust me with such an awesome responsibility was a gift I have always cherished. I do have to say, though, that as I rode up to my house that evening, my brother Jim behind me, the look on my mother's face could not be hidden. It was a look of great relief and "Oh my gosh, what was I thinking!"

CHAPTER 5

ARE WE THERE YET?
(THE SETTING)

Please indulge me, at this time, as I share with you a poem I wrote in honor of my little one-room country school and its impression it made not only on my life but also on all lives that were blessed to be a part of what took place on the grounds and in the building. We proudly exclaimed then, just as we do now, that we went to school at "Scotland School." No, I am not a poet, but what is written in the poem is true and foundational to my life.

Uphill One Way

A poem by Raymond L. Dykens, graduate of Scotland School.

Off we go on uphill slope, taking a path we've followed before.
A trail of anticipation and hope; we aren't rich, but neither are
we poor.
There it is, flying so high, its stars and stripes in full view.
Sunbeams streaming from the sky, it welcomes me and
welcomes you.

Finally we arrive, and we are all in line.
Hands over hearts and standing tall, allegiance we pledge,
Not to brag, but to honor a flag that never will fall.
I was proud then and proud today of its promise to us all.

Now we march in, each by their desk,
Standing in rows straight, proud, and neat.
And before we sit, ready to do our best,
The Bible verse from yesterday we now repeat.

So begins our day at Scotland School.
My class is finally in the eighth-grade row.
Each class their own row is the general rule.
Soon I will graduate and to a new school go.

But for now, I must study and learn.
The big test is coming, at which I must excel
If I am to become what I most yearn—
And whatever that is, I can't yet tell.

This day, as all days, are filled full:
Reading, writing, arithmetic, and more.
It's a goal we can all reach if we will all pull.
It's always fun to see what the day has in store.

The morning groups are organized and assembled.
It begins: the learning of spelling, science, math, and reading.
The teacher is near our row, and now we must show
What to our brains we have been feeding.

If we don't quite get it, she isn't as proud.
With patience, she has us try it some more.
It's seems she is trying to please the crowd.
Finally we see it like the light on the shore.

With diploma in hand, here I go. I am on my way.
I learned in my mind but was taught with heart.
I owe you so much for giving me this day.
Thank you, Scotland School, for giving me my start.

In those days, I may have described my arrival at school with these words: "There it is. That's my school." Now I would describe it more like a Norman Rockwell painting—simple but real, colorful but plain, exciting and promising. The building was a structure perhaps a little atypical for its time. Most one-room schools were constructed of wood. Scotland Elementary School was red brick with white board trim. On the east side was a bank of windows that ran nearly the entire length of the building. You can imagine the pros and cons of this design. It was cold in the winter, hot in the summer, hard to keep clean, and provided students a great view of the prairie. I never appreciated the scene that stretched out before me as I sat in the eighth-grade row, next to the windows, until now. It now is a picture in my mind of waving prairie grasses, sunrises, jackrabbits, sleigh rides, deer, a winter wonderland, and the harvest of hay. On the other hand, these windows provided us with a wonderful natural lighting system. The teacher had about a 90 percent view of the playground. I won't talk about what was happening in the other 10 percent. Oh, I may talk about some of it, but if I do, it will only be the truth.

On the southeast corner of the building, not attached but close, was a single-car garage with a coal bin along one side. The structure was of native stone commonly known as "big rocks." It was well built and provided a place for the teacher's car (long before her time, it would have stored her carriage), a hoop for shooting baskets, and a place to hide behind.

South and east of the garage stood a concrete-block outhouse for boys. I kid you not; it was at least fifty yards from the garage. It was well constructed, and as I recall, it was a three-hole facility. And I am honest when I say it came equipped with a Sears and Roebuck catalog. It also came with a seasonal black snake, a couple of black widow spiders, and a garden spider or two. I am not sure how all that worked in the ecosystem of life. I just know I never bothered them and they never bothered me. It also provided us a place where we could climb up high enough to step out onto our very high homemade stilts. I'll tell you more about the stilts later.

Northeast of the garage was another outhouse. It was exactly like the one just described. Of course, it belonged to the girls. Now, I don't know about the spiders or snakes, but supposedly the girls had real toilet paper, and it was a varmint-free facility. This was gossip, and I suspect it was made up just to make us boys mad. It, too, was at least fifty yards from the school. And of course both outhouses were downhill from the school. Now that is good engineering. The girls' facility, unlike the boys' facility, was clearly visible to the teacher from those famous east windows. That was a good thing, I think. It fact, it is probably the reason the black snake lived in ours.

The front of the building faced the west. Just north and west of the main entrance was our flagpole. Southwest of the main entrance, just on the other side of the driveway, was a large oak tree. South of this tree, maybe fifty feet, stood the water pump. Yes, it was a manual pump with a circle drive bordering it on the west side. It was a neat circle drive, as it went by the pump, went under the tree, came close to the main entrance, and met the road just south of the flagpole. I am sure I never appreciated it then, but what a welcoming picture it presented as we arrived each morning to our little one-room country school on the prairie.

This little one-room school stood proudly on the edge of a beautiful prairie. Its location, as the crow flies, was about three miles from Duenweg, Missouri. And as mentioned earlier, it was a little over one and a half miles from the Scotland community. Most of the students attending Scotland Elementary School, probably two thirds of them, lived in the community of Scotland. The rest of the student population lived in the surrounding area, within a radius of about two and a half to three miles. Boundaries did exist and were controlled by the county superintendent as to which schools students would attend. I am not sure where they were and am fairly confident they were not strictly enforced or complied with. Kind of like today, isn't it?

However, Duenweg had a much larger school and even had school buses. These buses ran through several one-room school districts. So, in the case of Scotland, a bus did come through our community, offering service to the Duenweg School System. As elementary students, we had a choice as to which school we wished to attend. But upon entering the ninth grade, we no longer had a choice. Duenweg had a high school, and of course Scotland did not. I did attend Duenweg Elementary for one year. I'll have more to tell of that experience and my return to the one-room country school later in the book. It was not a bad experience, but I have to say that it was much different and I preferred Scotland Elementary School.

Yes, our little school was not conveniently located, and it had its challenges, but we never once thought of it as being bad. It was just the way it was. It was much like being at home with a bunch of kids. As we drove up to the school, it was not unusual to see a bunch of chalk eraser outlines on the brick—testimony that some of us had been sent out to clean the chalk dust off the erasers. I am sure we didn't appreciate it as much as we should have, but on the other hand, I don't remember being disappointed or ashamed of my school. We loved it!

The flagpole was situated to the left of this picture. I sure wish it had been in this photo, as it was a most important part of our day. The cover of the book better illustrates its importance. If you look closely, you can see the garage at the back end of the school, on the right side. Just in front this garage and alongside the school was our dodgeball court. This area also served as a lunchtime hangout because it had both sun and shade and was not visible from inside the school. On the front of this garage was our basketball hoop. You can't see it, but it was our basketball court. We played Annie over using the roof of the school. In front of this building each year, we took an all-school picture. I have been able to collect many of these but of course not all of them. I hope some of you get to find yourselves in these pictures. They are indeed a story in and of themselves. Picture, if you can, the circle drive coming up in front of the front door, from your right to left. It went by the pump, under the tree, and out to the main road directly in front of the school. This image is portrayed through the painting that serves as the cover of this book.

I believe this would be a good time in my book to insert all of these school photos. One of them is not included here but is featured later in the book. It is a classic. Enjoy! The first one takes us back to 1921. I hope you can make out some names. I count thirty-one. It is interesting to note that the building is not the same one as pictured in my book. I believe it is in the same spot, but I'm not sure. Regardless, it gives us a glimpse into the beginnings of the importance of an education. It had to have been much like the TV series *Little House on the Prairie*, which most are familiar with. It is also interesting to note that the number of students enrolled was not that much different from the rest of the pictures I'll share with you. It is equally interesting to note that none of the boys are shirtless. That story is coming up. There are a few names that are very familiar to me, as they are the same last names of several people in the Scotland community, where I grew up. Pim, Snyder, Endicott, and Harper are all names that were stalwarts in my community. Add to these the others in my community that come to mind but are not pictured in the above photograph, and you have a group of Scotland neighbors that supported our school, our community, and, especially, the kids of that community. I'll probably forget some, but I'll run the risk and name a few more. The Longs, Kendricks, Summers, Chrismans, Bakers, Dykenses, Carters, Sampsons, Wormingtons, Trentons, Gaddis, and others who came and went all contributed to a village that raised children. Good job, Lola Kirk, you had a good-looking bunch.

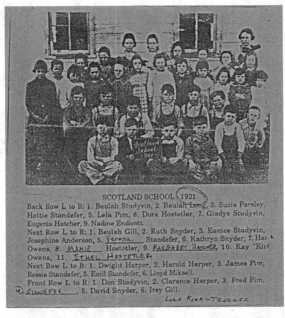

SCOTLAND SCHOOL 1921
Back Row L to R: 1. Beulah Studyvin, 2. Beulah Long, 3. Susie Parsley, Hattie Standefer, 5. Lela Pim, 6. Dora Hostetler, 7. Gladys Studyvin, Eugenia Hatcher, 9. Nadine Endicott.
Next Row L to R: 1. Beulah Gill, 2. Ruth Snyder, 3. Eunice Studyvin, Josephine Anderson, 5. Verena Standefer, 6. Kathryn Snyder, 7. Har Owens, 8. Mamie Hostetler, 9. Margaret Hatcher, 10. Kay "Kirk" Owens, 11. Ethel Hostetler.
Next Row L to R: 1. Dwight Harper, 2. Harold Harper, 3. James Pim, Rossie Standefer, 5. Emil Standefer, 6. Lloyd Miksell.
Front Row L to R: 1. Don Studyvin, 2. Clarence Harper, 3. Fred Pim, Standefer, 5. David Snyder, 6. Irey Gill.
Lola Kirk - Teacher

1921

1944-1945

1946-1947

1948-1949

1949-1950

1950-1951

1953-1954

1955-1956

1956-1957

1957-1958

1959-1960

The above photos are all I could come up with. Credit for my having these goes mostly to my mom. She purchased pictures every year she had children in Scotland Elementary School. That would be nine years. Others were given to me by classmates from their collections. They are wonderful and historical landmarks of a time gone by. In every one I see pride, worth, discipline, happiness, cleanliness, fun, respect, kids doing their best, and the community of Scotland raising kids. Included in some of these pictures (i.e., the photos of the class of 1955/56 and the class of 1956/57) are the two teachers I had during my Scotland Elementary School experience. The class picture of 1955/56 shows Lou Jamison. Zoe Wommack is in the 1956/57 class picture. I might add that, years later, she had former students serve as her pallbearers. I was honored to be one. These two ladies were difference-makers in my life. I am proud to have been one of their students.

CHAPTER 6

ENTER, PLEASE (INSIDE AND OUTSIDE LAYOUT)

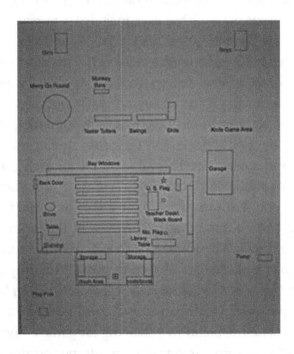

As one entered the building from the west side, one stepped into a small room called the cloakroom. It consisted of a table with a bucket of water for washing hands, a wash pan, and a dipper for drinking. No, we were not allowed to use the dipper for drinking.

But I will admit that I saw it happen more than once. Actually, the drinking water was in a separate bucket. This was back in the day but was not *Little House on the Prairie*. Each student had a glass with his or her name on it. I am not going to lie to you, since I have promised these to be true stories. The truth is that it was not uncommon for us to not use our glasses and to just use the dipper.

On one side of this entryway was a place to hang our coats and store our boots. On the other side of the space was a place to store our lunches brought from home. This little room was used for many purposes, including as a time-out discipline room. The teachers didn't call it "time-out" then, though; they just said, "Get in that room, and stay there until I tell you that you can come out." In addition, this room also served as "off stage left" for our school plays. It was also a shield, for the main room, from the cold air coming in through the front door. Other uses included a nurse's station (no, we did not have a nurse, just a cot for the ill) and a meeting room for upper-class meetings (eighth grade only). This entryway allowed us to enter the main schoolroom from the west side. It presented a picture that will forever live in my mind. As we entered, the first thing we saw, right in front of us, was a row of desks. These were reserved for the first graders. On the other side of the first-grade row were seven more rows. This allowed one for each grade. At the back of the room (the north end) was a coal stove, some bookshelves, and another door leading outside. The door was located in the very northeast corner of the room. In the front of the room (the south end) was the teacher's desk and chair, a piano, some more shelving, a library table, a blackboard that extended all the way across the room, a US flag, and a Missouri flag. The alphabet, in both lower case and upper case, was displayed above the blackboard, and off to one side opposite the piano was shelving for games. The space left after moving a few things to one side was our performing arts stage.

On the east side of the room, just beyond the eighth-grade row of desks, was the bay of windows I spoke of earlier. Add to this picture a wooden floor, wooden runners under the desks, a few folding chairs near the coal stove used for huddling around the fire, some light fixtures hanging overhead on long chains, and you have a layout that looks something like the above drawing. A few of my classmates may remember it differently, and they very well could be right. Things did get moved around quite a bit because of the need to adjust for occasions such as pie suppers, inside games, and performances, or maybe just for a change. I do believe, however, the desks and row designations remained pretty much the same over the years. A drawing in no way can ever express the way we looked at it. To me it felt safe and right, like a home away from home. Yes, I am confident I speak for most Scotland alumni when I say we were proud of our school.

The following pictures are not pictures of Scotland Elementary School. They are shared as a courtesy of the Community of Christ Historic Liberty Hall Property in Lamoni, Iowa. The school is an actual school that sits on their property, and it has been maintained over these many years as an important piece of our history. It is toured often by visitors and used often by local schools for field trips. It provides them with a taste of what it was like to be a student in a one-room country school. While the furniture differs somewhat from the furniture used in Scotland Elementary School, the desks are very similar. Their desks also had inkwells and generally were of the same design. Ours, however, were on runners, which made it easier to move them and to clean the floor. I can provide personal testimony about this because during my eighth-grade year I was the janitor. I will speak to that experience later in the book. The blackboards were of the same material, but our blackboard was located at the front of the room instead of the back of the room. The bookcases were very similar, but we had at least three of those. Compared to Scotland Elementary School, this is a much smaller school and from an era much earlier than Scotland Elementary School's construction. The teacher's desk is smaller. I am glad we still have examples of the one-room school for our young folks to get a glimpse of in order to better appreciate their heritage.

Student desks

potbellied stove

blackboard

Notice the inkwells in the student desks. We had these in our desks, but they had been out of use since the invention of the cartridge-fill ink pens and then ballpoint pens. Personally, I still like to use my number 2 pencil and a Big Chief tablet. I will say our map was very similar to the one pictured, and more importantly, it was used a bunch. I have a feeling we knew more geography than most people gave us credit for. And if we didn't, it wasn't because the opportunity to learn it wasn't present. That's kind of like learning today, isn't it? I believe so. Just having it in front of us isn't enough. We still need to perfect the art of learning how to apply it. But in spite of what you may interpret as my negative attitude toward learning, I believe we are better than ever before and getting better with each new generation. From what I see coming out of our students in 2018, I feel our future is in good hands.

A VIEW FROM ROW ONE (LET'S HEAR FROM A FORMER SCOTLAND FIRST GRADER)

The following story is included in memory of my brother, Charles R. Dykens (Bob). He submitted it and authored it, and I am proud to include it. He attended Scotland for only one year, but it did make an impact on him, as you will be able to tell from his perception of what it was like being a first grader at Scotland Elementary School.

*****

I had the world by the tail upon reaching the ripe old age of five and being solely in charge of all fun activities at our house. Sure, I missed my brothers when they headed off to school, but I had Pinky Lee, Howdy Doody, and Captain Kangaroo to accompany me through each day's journey. For the most part, life at home was smooth sailing: eating chocolate mayonnaise cupcakes and taking naps in the nice, warm sunroom. Life as I knew it, however, changed one afternoon in September 1957. Instead of taking my usual nap, Mom decided to teach me my ABCs, numbers, and how to sign my name. I never put it together until years later, but I distinctly remember Mom and the teacher having a conversation about me when she was dropping off my brothers at school one morning. I knew I had another year of Pinky Lee and Howdy Doody to enjoy, as I was only five and had to be six to start the first grade, right? Wrong. It is all too clear now that a plot had been laid against Howdy Doody and me because the ABCs replaced the afternoon nap that very day.

Well, the next morning came, and life as I knew it had ended. It was all a blur, but I was dressed, fed, equipped with a Big Chief tablet, a pencil, and a Roy Rogers lunchbox as I joined the ranks of the other inmates and trudged off to school.

Still unsure as to what to do when I got to school, I must have had a deer-in-the-headlights look about me as I gazed upon the wonder of it all. There were kids of every size. Some were tall, and some were as tall as trees. The teacher gave me a desk near the door, and I caught a glimpse of my dear mom as she silently left the school building. Had it not been for my brother seated only a few rows away, my days of breathing likely would have come to an end. The teacher must have seen the tears welling up in my eyes, as she leaned down and talked me back into a reality I could live with. The teacher with a broad smile was kind to me from that day forward. She made me feel at home, and although she had a gentle spirit, she garnered a respect from all children, and adults as well.

One particular memory of her astounding character and grit came early one morning when a fellow first grader came to school smoking a pipe. Now, understand that at age five, I did not possess all worldly understanding, but I had managed to collect enough reasoning skills, at that early age, to know that there was something wrong with that picture. The teacher must have shared those same skills with me, because she was instantly up from her desk, had the pipe out of his mouth, and began a scolding on that boy that would cow any man. To fully explain the story, however, I have to describe his appearance. He was big for a first grader, likely the result of having been held back a year or two, and was somewhat chubby. He was dressed in a checkered shirt made from a cloth like one you might find on your grandma's table. Over the shirt he had a fair-looking pair of bib overalls—the kind we often saw on the first day of school when wear and tear had not yet set in. I don't remember much about his shoes, because in those days, shoes were sometimes optional. It all depended on something Mom and Dad referred to as "hard times."

Anyway, returning to the story, the teacher confiscated the still-warm pipe and placed it on her desk. I concluded that this first grader had given up smoking and the teacher had made her point. However, the next morning, a giant of a man showed up at school with this same young classmate trailing close in his shadow. This fellow was dressed exactly like my earlier description—checkered shirt and overalls—but not quite as tidy. This man's belly seemed to be adrift outside the limits of his shirt and bibs. In addition, he could have done a great service to his shirt, his bibs, and the fragrance of that schoolroom, if he had waded neck deep through the creek on his way to school that morning. At any rate, one of the most impressive sights to see came next, when that kind old teacher looked up at the fellow and said, "Your boy is not allowed to come to school smoking a pipe." Dad snorted and bellowed out in a Santa Claus–style voice, "If my boy wants to smoke a pipe, he can smoke a pipe." With that said, the kind, experienced teacher replied, "Well, he is not smoking a pipe here, and you can leave now, as I have a school to attend to." I never saw my classmate or his daddy again, and no one from that day forward felt the compulsion to ever try to smoke at school.

As important as reading and writing are, there are things at school that require greater attention, at times, than reading about Spot, Dick, or Jane. Probably first and foremost is knowing where the bathroom is. The bathrooms were located a far cry from the school building, and for a first grader, this became a serious matter. Besides the smells and an occasional black snake associated with the school's outdoor privies, the distance created a concern for a five-year-old student not knowing exactly when to raise his hand for permission to go. Again the wisdom of our kind teacher came out, as she assigned an eighth grader to accompany a first grader who had such a need. Firsthand experience can relay to you now that a child being hurried to the outhouse by an older student has a much better chance of being on time than one left to his own demise and wits. My particular guardian angel was a fellow named Bob, but we called him "Crows' Feet Crow." I have no idea as to how he got that name, as there was nothing particularly special about Bob's feet. He did have notoriety and some class distinction, however, which came from his ability to always win at playing various games. He seemed to always win. Looking back on that, I wonder if everything was on the up-and-up.

Another important challenge to overcome about being at school was eating lunch. Mom always had our lunches packed, and we could easily count on a biscuit or homemade light bread with peanut butter, whole cow's milk, and a piece of cake. We would gather on the south side of the stone building where the horses use to be stabled (now the garage) and sit in the sun while eating our lunches. Most kids had lunches similar to ours, but there was one boy whose mom owned a food store, so his lunches were an education in and of themselves. I witnessed firsthand store-bought bread, sliced bologna, cheese, lettuce, potato chips, and Hostess Twinkies as regular entrées laid out before us. Needless to say, we all tried our skills at trading, but the bounty we offered rarely caught the attention of ole Crows' Feet Crow, the store owner's son.

Not to be forgotten on the list of knowledge essentials concerning first-grade life at the one-room country school was an activity we called recess. Recess had a way of erasing the tyranny and numbness of being attached to a wooden bench for hours on end, listening to the same story about Dick and Jane and a dog named Spot. The way I figured it, Spot must have been a city dog, as all he did was run and jump. However, that alone always seemed to excite Dick and Jane, who made a great deal of it all. I have no idea what Dick and Jane would have done had they met up with our dog, Corky. Corky was the best snake-killing, squirrel-treeing, and fighting dog in our part of the country. Noted for his crooked neck, which had been broken as a result of chasing cars, Corky would have easily put Spot in his place.

At any rate, recess was an important part of my education. I learned games and rhymes, made friends, learned new words, and was introduced to the greatest game ever—baseball. However, at age five, I rarely was allowed to play. But that did not stop me from studying the game. Just choosing sides and who got first picks and first at bats was a game in itself. One of the captains would toss a bat to the captain of the other team. He would catch it somewhere along the handle. The one who tossed the bat would then stack his hand on top of the hand of the one who caught it. They would continue stacking hands until there was only a small portion of the bat handle showing. Now, this is where it got interesting. If the captain whose hands were free could somehow force two fingers onto the knob of the bat and clutch the bat firmly enough, the other captain would release his hand for the final test. The final test was for the captain clutching the knob to swing the bat backward over his shoulder for a distance of ten feet. This sounds like a lengthy process, and as intriguing as it was, the whole thing lasted only about a minute. Both girls and boys played, and it took all able bodies in the school to field a team. Sometimes parents would show up at school and we would all travel to another area school for a ball game. There were some pretty fair ballplayers, both boys and girls, as I recall.

There are simply too many memories to list, but in selecting these few, I hope I have given you a glimpse of what life was like at a one-room country school through the eyes of a first grader.

Bob Dykens

*****

SCOTLAND HOME
BoB HoME IN SCOTLAND.

CHAPTER

8

LIFE CHANGERS: TEACHERS CALLED TO BE TEACHERS

I was so blessed to have had teachers in my life—especially those in this little one-room country school who were truly called to be teachers. They have all given me something I needed. But getting one's education off to a good start, at least in my professional opinion, requires teachers, in the primary grades especially, who are just plain gifted and called to serve at that level. I am most fortunate to have experienced these types of teachers early in my educational career as a student. They were understanding, compassionate, loving, and fair but firm. No, I am not talking about a slap across the knuckles with a ruler, although that certainly was in the realm of possibility. My teachers were indeed masters at getting their students involved in the teaching process. They realized that through this process, students had a much better opportunity to learn.

Think about it. In my case, I took several American history courses during the tenure of my formal education, including college. But I never really learned American history until I taught it to high school students at Golden City High School in Golden City, Missouri. I wasn't even certified to teach it, but I did have enough hours to qualify for a temporary certificate. In my early days of teaching, this was not an uncommon practice. I sincerely hope, to this day, I didn't harm that bunch of students too much. I did my best and learned along with them, and I suspect they all survived in spite of my lack of knowledge and experience. I went on as a school administrator to adhere to the philosophy that we learn best when we are put into a position to teach others. I have had the honor, as a high school principal, to train many beginning teachers under this framework. As a parent, educator, supervisor, and leader, I hope you agree. If not, try it. It works.

I had better get back to my story. Sorry about that. Yes, my teachers in this one-room country school were good disciplinarians. Even in my early grades at Scotland Elementary School, I realized the discipline they handed out was always served with love and compassion. They insisted on an environment they could best teach in and we, as students, could best learn in. We learned at a very early age to respect that standard. They loved "their children," and—trust me—in some cases, that was a challenge. They taught us all: the poor, the not so clean, the smart, the fast, and the slow, and they taught us that every one of us could be successful. Special education meant we were "all special." We each had our own gifts and abilities to learn. Eight grades met in one room every day. Any given year would see a population of twenty to thirty-five students seated in those eight rows of desks. Every day would begin with this same population of students gathered around the flagpole, standing at attention with hands over hearts as we prepared to salute the flag of our great country. It was instilled in us to march into that school and to do our best. I truly believe that we were never plotting to see what we could get away with as we entered into our house of not just study but also fun. As far as we were concerned, our teacher was "Super Teacher." This attitude of respect, of course, began with our teachings at home. We bought into the idea that we were on her side. We would have done anything for her. Every teacher I had made a positive difference in my life.

Remember: we are all teachers, and we can all make a positive difference in the lives of the students who surround us on a daily basis. Little eyes are watching, and little ears are listening. Use good judgment. If I could incorporate into this writing all the teachers (in and out of the classroom) I've had over my years, it would cover many, many pages about positive impact on my life. They were all good teachers and deserve my sincere thanks. Having said that, I will admit that while they were all good teachers, some were better than others. That was to my advantage because it challenged me to work harder and to stay positive. As I have shared with my teachers while I was in the role of an administrator, it is critical that we put our very best efforts into the elementary grades, being sure that all students develop a love for learning at a very early age.

These were not only my teachers; they were my friends, and they truly did develop in me a love for learning. They were different yet all the same in their quest to do the best for their students. Perhaps there are those who would argue against my praise of these instructors. If so, I've never met them. Oh, we had our moments, but when the dust settled, we talked, we learned, and we even agreed to disagree. We knew our parents would be supportive and would be fair with all those involved in any situation. That's just the way it was in my one-room country school.

Zoe Wommack was my teacher for the first, second, fourth, fifth, and some of the eighth grades. This lady was indeed gifted! When I was in the first grade, I developed a very serious stuttering problem. She spent endless hours with me before and after school. By the time I was halfway through my second-grade year, she had taught me how not to stutter. I don't know any other way to put it. I just know that without her intervention, I may very well have stuttered throughout my entire life. I truly believe that. I owe so much to her and am most positive that without her influence, I would not have had the educational experiences I enjoyed during the rest of my life. I was, as a grown adult, honored to be one of the pallbearers at her funeral. I learned from her the basics of leadership and responsibility.

Mrs. Setser was my third-grade teacher at Duenweg Elementary. Duenweg was a much larger school than Scotland and was so big that the third graders had their own room. It was the only year of my first eight grades that I did not attend Scotland Elementary School. But that is another story for another time. I will say that I liked a lot of what it had to offer, but it seemed so awfully big. Riding the big, yellow bus was fun. A prohibition on spitting and picking one's nose, as well as a requirement of saying "yes, ma'am," "no, ma'am," "may I," "please," "thank you," and so forth, were major parts of the curriculum in her third-grade room. As I stated earlier, every teacher I've ever had has provided me with something I needed to learn. Thank you, Mrs. Setser! I must confess I never perfected all these, although I could spit pretty well.

There is one other story I wish to share from my third-grade experience at Duenweg. Valentine's Day was special, and we were all to bring valentine cards. A time was set for each of us to get up from our desk, one at a time, and pass out our cards to our friends. I got a few, some got a bunch, and a few got only one or two. I remember feeling bad about that. I am not blaming my teacher, as it was the practice for all grades in the school to do it this way. Later in life, I relived this experience as it hit close to my doorstep. I was the principal of a high school, and it was the custom on Valentine's Day that cards, flowers, and gifts arrived all through the day. It was a small community, and to stop this tradition would hurt the local flower shops. So, in an effort to at least control them, we placed them on tables outside the office and allowed those for whom they were intended to come pick them up during the last fifteen minutes before the end of the school day. It was sad when I realized this was no different than what I had experienced on Valentine's Day as a third grader. We even had students who sent flowers to themselves so they wouldn't be left out. I felt so responsible for this wrong. There had to have been a better way. I apologize for digressing from my one-room country school stories, but I felt I had to share this account. Is this still happening in our society today? Of course it is! And it probably always will. Please don't blame the schools. Parents, we have to be the mentors of our own children. At any rate, I returned to Mrs. Wommack for my fourth- and fifth-grade years.

I had Lou Jamison, a wonderful teacher, for my sixth-, seventh-, and eighth-grade years. She was truly a great teacher. She taught kids, not subjects. She not only made sure that our minds were challenged, but, equally important, also challenged our souls and encouraged us to take care of our bodies. One thing I want to be sure to mention about this lady is her dramatics abilities. She was a gifted actress. She would often put skits on for us in which she would portray a character; usually it was a portrayal of drama. She even did these for the community programs. The whole community loved these performances. She was very, very good.

Of course there were other teachers who had a tremendous influence on the students of Scotland Elementary School. If we could speak with students before the tenures of these teachers I was blessed with, we would find, I am sure, the same amount of dedication, love, and desire that all children be educated to the best of their abilities. I salute them and thank them for their contributions in paving the way for my experiences. I say to them as well, *thank you.*

PICTURE DAY (SHIRTLESS)

The following story was submitted and authored by my brother, James "Jim" William Dykens. It is one of his favorite memories of the little schoolhouse on the prairie.

*****

I attended Scotland Elementary during grades one through five. After all these years and three college degrees later, I am convinced that my years at Scotland provided me with a good foundation necessary to be successful. I can't remember, but one bad day at school, I missed my mom, and so I ran away from school. I received my first whipping! And that is all I have to say about that!

Ms. Jamison and Ms. Wommack were both good teachers. While I was not a strong student, I enjoyed all the enrichment we experienced. My favorite activity was playing softball against other schools. It was a big deal. Other schools I remember playing against are Stony Point, Underwood, Perseverance, and Warren's Branch. There were probably others. My dad even took off work to attend many of these games. Winter would mean lots of snow, which meant some special activities were going to happen. Chili day was one of my favorites. My very favorite, though, was when Shorty Baker, one of our school patrons, would bring his tractor and huge sled to school and give us rides around the prairie.

Lots of cold lunches brought from home didn't seem to hurt anyone. With eight grades in one room and only one teacher, we were close to each other. Older kids were often tasked with helping the younger ones. In today's schools, we use fancy terms like "cooperative learning," "peer tutoring," "multitasking," "brainstorming," and "lifelong learning." We just called it "school." And finally I'll share with you my most embarrassing moment.

One day only, during the school year, we were allowed to not wear a shirt to school. Little did I know that John Gaddis and Jim Dykens would pick picture day as their day to bare their chests.

******

Note: I, too, am in this picture that Jim submitted as evidence of his most embarrassing moment. I have no explanation for my lack of leadership on his behalf. After all, I was the big brother and should have looked out for his well-being. He has probably wondered that himself over the years. I wish I could say that I was just too busy with early-morning chores and therefore missed checking on him. But I can't. I really don't remember what happened. But if I had thought to do it, I would have taken my shirt off too. At least we both would have been in the same pickle. Sorry, Jim; I am just a slow thinker. Seriously, it is a great memory for both of us, and as you can probably guess, the teacher did not make a big deal out of it. By the way, Jim is the one in the second row on the end.

1953-1954

PLAYGROUND EQUIPMENT (FOR REAL)

For the most part, our playground equipment was either homemade or remade many times over by volunteers in the community. I regret that I do not have the actual pictures of our playground, but I do have pictures of playgrounds very similar to the one we enjoyed. I will say it was properly taken care of, in good working order, and clean, and as many safety standards as possible were employed. By today's standards, we would not have been allowed to play on some of it. I'll briefly share with you the ups and downs of this equipment and hope that for many of you it brings back good memories. Speaking of the ups and downs, I would say that the teeter-totters would be a good place to start.

Teeter-Totters

The teeter-totters were some kind of fun. Yes, they could be a little dangerous—especially if you couldn't trust your partner. As I recall, we had four of these. They were strongly built of wood and steel, and maintained with yearly coats of paint. They were indeed used by all grades extensively. Those in the below image are not the ones at Scotland but look very much like them.

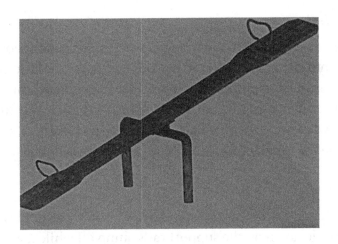

Merry-Go-Round

Like the teeter-totters, this machine was much fun, but it did have its drawbacks as well. It was a good way to get sick if you could stay on and a good way to get hurt if you got off too quickly. You know the kind of merry-go-round I speak of. It was sort of an umbrella-looking affair. The path around it was deep from the pushing we did as we ran beside it. It provided many games for all ages. We sort of had rules and understandings that applied to all grade levels. They went something like this.

Grades 1–3

These grades enjoyed nice, easy, and slow rides with supervision. They waited until it stopped to get off. Big kids made sure the little ones got their turns in an appropriate manner. I have mentioned this big kid / little kid relationship before, and it is true. I think it was that way because when we were little kids, we were treated that way, and thus it became the standard for us all. Now why can't we do that today?

Grades 4–6

Fast, fast, and faster was the standard. Kids in these grades would hang upside down on the support rails, jump off while it was going fast, and try to stay on their feet. They would get on while it was moving, but only if grades 1–3 were already on it. Read "Grades 1–3" again if you don't understand.

Grades 7–8

"Faster, faster, faster!" was the cry. Kids in these grades would stand on it without holding on while it was going full speed. They would get on at full speed and later get off at full speed and enjoy a good tumble and roll on the grass of the Scotland prairie. I am not sure how it could be such a nice piece of playground equipment and at the same time such an unforgiving experience. Obviously, some of these tactics had to be employed when the teacher was on the other side of the building. We used lookouts. That is the truth. I didn't say we were angels. The merry-go-round in the above picture is not the one that was at Scotland but is very similar in construction. Actually, as I recall, ours had a wooden deck. But I couldn't pass this one up, as the characters on it are my four grandchildren: Dixie, Bode, Sevi, and Ellie. I know it is not in character with the times I write about, but nonetheless, the story is true. What is in character about this picture is that they enjoyed playing on it just as much as I did, and I suspect the merry-go-rounds of today get that same respect.

Swings

These, too, are not the swings we had at Scotland, but they are very similar in that they are made of wood and metal, which as I recall worked very well for bailing out at the highest point possible. This was fun but is not advisable.

Monkey Bars

These were my favorite. Ours were a simple set of a single line of bars at three different heights. We called them monkey bars, but a better term would have been "chin-up bars." Ours were a little narrower than the ones shown but built pretty much the same by the good dads of the community of Scotland. I was not sure exactly how one was to play on them, but I can tell you how not to play on them.

How Not to Play on Them

On one occasion, it was the top height that did me in. I was playing on the monkey bars while admittedly enjoying the attention of a couple of girls. What better chance than this to show off my athletic skills? Anyway, I had been put out of the knock-down-and-drag-out game early, so why not build up my ole biceps a little, right? I really am not sure how it happened. I do know it happened quickly. I am thinking it probably happened during my attempt to do a double twist, reverse, upside down toehold. Whatever it was, I slipped! I took one right in the smacker. Yep, the top bar of the highest height was inserted squarely into my mouth. My two upper front teeth were now hanging down over my lower lip, attached only by their roots. Needless to say, the blood was pouring. I remember holding them in my hand to keep them from falling all the way out while I ran seeking help from the teacher. You would have thought the two girls who were watching this would have already gone after her. I guess it wasn't all that impressive, or maybe they thought it was funny. I don't know. But I do know that my teacher, bless her heart, was everything. She was not only a great teacher; she was also a great nurse when she had to be. I was in hysterics. I was crying loudly, screaming, and really scared. She took one look at me, grabbed my two dangling teeth, and shoved them back into the hole they came out of. (I don't think even real certified nurses have this training, do they?) I'll never forget her words to me as she firmly said, "If your dad could survive WWII, you can survive this. Shut up and let me help you!" I did, and she did. I don't remember it hurting when she shoved them back into place.

By the time she had the teeth in place, she had already sent a runner to my house with the news. (Remember: we didn't have a phone in the school. She did have her car, but she didn't dare to leave. Leaving the kids alone was not an option.) Remember the name of this book? *Uphill One Way.* The good news is that the downhill part was the trip from the school to home, so that helped the runner a good deal. I really don't remember who the runner was. I am sure it was probably a seventh or eighth grader. I am now seventy-four as I finish writing this book, and I still have those same two teeth. One of them is dead and a little off color, but they are still strong enough to eat an apple. I sure hope I thanked my teacher for giving them a good shove.

As my mother and I arrived at the dentist, I remember how pleased he was that my teacher had done what she did. Thank you, Lou Jamison. I believe, with all my heart, that this lady still watches over her students from above.

Basketball

Okay, time to move on to another piece of playground equipment. It must have been a good one because I don't remember it ever getting changed. I know it didn't during my tenure. Of course, there wasn't much dunking going on, so it got zero wear and tear from that skill. We played our basketball games on that same gravel I spoke of that served as our dodgeball arena. Our rim was mounted on the end of the rock garage. I've already described the layout of this fine garage and coal bin. I don't believe we played much team basketball, if any. I don't remember any. We played a lot of horse and mainly just shot baskets. Maybe it was because we had very few tall kids and the rim was the full ten-foot height. Anyway, we only had one ball, and it was usually flat from being used as a dodgeball. I guess we weren't a basketball school. I wish I could tell you a story of how I shot five hundred shots a day at that rim and went on to play college basketball, but I can't. I do wish I had given basketball a better effort at this age, but then again, dodgeball sure was a lot of fun.

OTHER GAMES (SOME REAL, SOME CREATED, ALL FUN)

Oh my goodness! We had a great time and sort of created games as we went along. You may recognize many of the following game names. Some you will not. Even if you recognize the name of a game, don't assume it to be the same one you remember playing. We did, for the most part, make up our own rules. And, of course, we made changes necessary to adapt to our particular setting and available participants. While the following are the games I liked and remember, not everyone will agree. But I am betting that in this chapter someplace is a game or two you either enjoyed or would have enjoyed.

Secondly, I wish to make the point that it is true that several people would be eliminated from these games quickly and be forced to wait until a new game started. This is where the playground equipment came in handy. Believe it or not, we had several neat pieces of equipment. This was largely because of the dads of the community. They built most of them, maintained them, and some even played on them when they were in school. And if they did not, their kids did. There were no grants for playground equipment, no safety standards, and no money to have someone hired to build it. But we had it, and we loved it. Let's take a quick peek at some of the games we played.

Knock-Down-and-Drag-Out

This was not a complicated game, which explains why I liked it. It was a game geared primarily for seventh and eighth graders but was open to all. It began, as many of our games did, by choosing sides. You already know how this goes. While it is somewhat fair to the game, it isn't always fair to the feelings of some of the participants. Of course, at that age, I guess I never gave that much thought, but I should have. Usually there were about twenty to thirty kids in the whole school, from grades one through eight. That meant that maybe half that many would let their names be chosen for participation in this game. Looking back on the process, there was, of course, some peer pressure going on as well. It was necessary to be sure we had a good game. Once we had established the two teams, we drew two parallel lines on the ground. As I recall, they were maybe twenty steps from each other. For people like me who need a visual, here it is:

Xs vs. Os

Team X Goal Line

X X 0 X
X 0
0 X 0 X 0 0
X 0
X 0 0 X

Team 0 Goal Line

Each team would then select a captain and huddle with their chosen leader. The purpose of this was to come up with a game plan. After a short time (recess was only fifteen or twenty minutes), both teams would gather inside the two lines. We just sort of knew who was on our team. (We usually kept the same teams for a week or so. This saved a lot of time and thus allowed for more actual playing time.) It started with one of the little kids, too young to participate, standing off to one side and yelling, "Go!" With that command, the game was on.

The object of the game was simple. Knock down an opponent and drag him or her across your line. One team owned line A, and one team owned line B. Once you were dragged across the line of your opponent, you could not return to the game; you were out—which, by the way, was a choice several were willing to submit to once the command to go was given. It was sort of a given that choosing to leave the game in this manner was a better choice than choosing not to be chosen in the first place.

The winner was the team with at least one member still standing between the lines. In case the bell ending recess rang before the game ended, the team with the most members still between the lines was declared the winner. In the case of a tie, the game would pick up at that point and continue at the next recess. It sounds simple, but there actually was a lot of strategy. One tactic was to gang up on the best player of the other team and get him or her out of there as soon as possible. It was a complicated strategy because the other team usually had the same thing in mind. I would draw you a diagram of this happening, but in no way would it or could it do justice to the actual encounter. You get the picture.

A game usually took only three or four minutes to play, and there were no time-outs. So, most of the time, we were able to get in two or three games before recess was over. All the strategy was worked out ahead of time. Yes, some of it was decided through the passing of notes during school. Since it was nearly impossible to stop a game once it had started, even though the bell was ringing, it became necessary to negotiate a solution to this problem. It was negotiated with our teacher, and she agreed to the following. If the game was in process at the ringing of the bell, we would be allowed to either finish that game or to call it a tie. It was our choice. Of course, we pretty much knew the bell schedule, so we made sure a game was in process when the bell rang. We had a great teacher. She knew the games would be short. And so, with our pulled-off buttons, torn shirts, sweat, and even, on occasion, some blood and tears, we headed to class. I know it sounds a little rough, but, believe it or not, we did not take cheap shots. We never intentionally hurt anyone, and we played fair. There was no referee, just a bunch of kids having a roughhouse game of knock-down-and-drag-out.

Mumblety-Peg

This game was also called mumbly-peg or mumble the peg; any of these names will get you to the right game. Unlike knock-down-and-drag-out, this was more of a quiet, gentle, and humbling game. It did require each participant to have a two-bladed pocketknife. (In today's world, this game would, of course, not be allowed.) The participants would position themselves in a circle. Perhaps as many as three or four would be in the same game. Each would take a turn at flipping his knife up and out into the circle. If it stuck into the ground with the big blade only, it was worth twenty-five points. The little blade was worth fifty points. And if one could stick it with both blades, he received one hundred points. The first person to get to five hundred points won the game. But winning wasn't the big deal. The loser (the one with the fewest points) had to "eat the peg." The peg was usually a matchstick. In those days, matchsticks were strong and also served as toothpicks. The winner of the game had the privilege of sticking one end of the matchstick in the ground. He would stick it in just far enough for it to stand on its own. Then, while holding the knife by the flat portion of the long blade, he would use the knife as a hammer. Three hits were allowed for the purpose of driving the matchstick as far into the ground as possible. For an experienced player, it was not hard to bury the matchstick below ground level. Regardless of how deep into the ground the matchstick was driven, it was the player with the fewest points who had to pull the peg from the ground. The catch was that he had to get the matchstick out of the ground by using only his teeth. So, with the teeth being used as a tool, up and out of the ground came the matchstick, usually along with a mouthful of dirt.

"What about the girls?" you may ask. I really don't remember ever being in a game of mumblety-peg with a girl as one of the participants. They played knock-down-and-drag-out but not mumblety-peg. It was probably because they did not carry knives, as the boys did. I do remember that I did offer to let them use mine if they wanted to play. Like I said, I don't remember any ever taking me up on that offer. As a participant myself, I indeed tasted the thrill of driving the peg far into the ground. And I also tasted good ole Mother Earth. Sort of like life, isn't it?

Yes, the game was silly, and while it did require some skill with a pocketknife, and perhaps a little math, I really can't endorse it as an activity that should have been allowed, even in those days. I know some of you are perhaps thinking right now, *Wait a minute; that is not the way we played mumblety-peg.* And I am sure you are correct. We called it by that name, and I am positive there are many, many variations of the same game.

In fact, I'll share with you another twist of that same game. In this version, the winner of the game not only got to drive the peg but also got to lead off the next game by announcing to us where we were to throw the knife from. It might be from the top of the head, behind the back, between the legs, or wherever he chose. After the first round of tosses, the one with the most points would dictate the position of the throw. It was a most interesting addition to our game, and needless to say, in the interest of safety, the circle enlarged in direct proportion to the complexity of the toss position. I loved this game, and the honest truth is that the one who had to pull the peg from the ground was always a good sport about it. In fact, it was not uncommon for the others to cheer the peg-puller on in his efforts. Having successfully accomplished the feat, the puller would often receive pats on the back. I guess one could say it was sort of an honor to be the peg-puller.

Please note that we were never able to negotiate more time to finish this particular game when the bell to go in interrupted it. On the other hand, this was one of those games best played out behind the garage and out of the view provided by the long line of windows. I am glad I had this experience, but to my grandkids and to all kids of all ages, please don't play with knives or eat dirt. It was not a smart thing for us to play this game, but it is the truth that we did.

Stretch Out

Oh boy, another knife game. This game was allowed, but with strict rules as to who could participate. Most of the time, we followed those rules. The game was played with two players facing each other toe-to-toe. A line was drawn out to each side, parallel to their toes. I will draw you a picture.

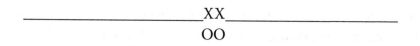

While this explanation is not a true description of the game I am explaining, it is as close as I could come up with. Use your imagination a little. Each of the two players would have their knife out with only the long blade open. The one chosen to throw first would launch his knife toward the line of his choice. If it stuck and was within six inches of the line, the other player would be required to keep one foot in place and stretch out with the other to the point of where the knife, just thrown by his opponent, had stuck in the ground. He was required to retrieve the knife and hand it back to his opponent, handle first. If he was able to accomplish this, he was then allowed to throw his knife toward the other line while still in his stretched-out position. The same rule applied. It had to stick and be within six inches of the line. If the opponent could retrieve it using the same game rules, the game continued and it was now the other guy's turn. The game went on until one or other could no longer reach the knife, retrieve it, and hand it back to his opponent without falling over.

Of course, going first was definitely an advantage. But you had to be careful. If you went first, it was really important that you got a "stick." This meant your opponent had to stretch out some before he could throw—at least to some degree. If you missed while going for a longer throw, it could cost you the game. On the other hand, the game could be won with only one throw. I also loved this game. I was built for it. I was skinny, had fair balance, and could throw some sticks at decent distances. But I was definitely not the best player. I got beaten fairly regularly, which forced me to get better and smarter at what I was trying to do. (Not a bad lesson for life, right?) I did get better and won just enough to keep me coming back. I had fun! And just like mumblety-peg, the loser had to pull the peg. Yep, from the dirt, with his teeth. Of course, this is not a game young boys play today—at least I hope not!

Dodgeball

Just like it was back in the day, dodgeball continues to be a favorite with children and, for that matter, adults as well. It was always one of my favorites as a student at Scotland Elementary School, Carterville High School, and even as a teacher of physical education during my tenure in several classrooms of southwest Missouri. I speak specifically of Jasper (my first teaching job), Golden City, and Stockton, Missouri. We played perhaps a little differently and with different rules, but in the end, we still had to dodge the ball. But Scotland was the best. We played it along the south side of the building. There were two reasons for this. First, there were no windows on that side, and also that side bordered the gravel driveway that led to the garage. This provided a suitable surface to play on. We had two versions.

One version was played from behind two lines, with players in between. This one was probably our favorite. It best fit our situation of having only two or maybe three playground balls at our disposal. The other version had a team throwing at a team lined up against the building from behind a line that was maybe twenty feet away.

The games could be played as a team sport, with one team in the middle and the other team behind the lines, throwing at them. The game was timed, and at the end of an allowed time, we simply counted the number remaining in the middle that had not yet been hit. Then we changed places and gave the other team their chance. If the game was played with individuals rather than teams, we would choose a pair to start out throwing, with everyone else in the middle. As people were hit, they would become throwers. If you started as a thrower, you got to move to the middle as soon as the first two were hit. The last one remaining in the middle was declared the champ. It was a real feat, and one that could be accomplished. I know it sounds impossible with everyone throwing at the last two or three, but remember: we only had two or three balls we were allowed to use.

The truth is that this game usually produced more injuries than knock-down-and-drag-out. There were times when the teacher would suspend the game because of the flow of blood. Most of the time, this was a result of falling down on the sharp gravel and rocks. I'm proud that only once was I the cause of a suspended game. With only two of us left in the middle, I fell and hit my head on a rock. The other guy argued that I should forfeit, but I never conceded, and we never finished the game. It took some time for the teacher to get the bleeding stopped.

Our version wasn't as sophisticated as the modern versions of dodgeball, but I assure you we had just as much fun. Maybe more!

Jacks

I can't believe I have gone from knock-down-and-drag-out to jacks. But hey, you have to have something to do on a rainy day. Believe me; if at all possible, our teacher wanted us outside at recess. I wonder why. Anyway, we would clear off the library table and start with our "onesies." It didn't matter; we played hard and competed with the same enthusiasm as when we were outside. Just like today's youth, we took most games way too seriously. "Were you any good at this game?" you may ask. Actually, I wasn't bad. While I never won a championship, I usually finished fairly high.

Remember those girls I mentioned earlier who didn't want to play mumblety-peg? Well, they were inside practicing jacks. There is, as many of you know, a real art in being able to pick them up. And even more important is how one throws them down. I never caught on exactly to how I should throw them down. I could get to my fours or fives maybe, but at that point, my level of competition diminished greatly. Again, some of you know exactly what I'm talking about, don't you?

*****

Puzzles, board games, and creative drawing on the blackboard were utilized and encouraged. Believe it or not, there were times when we just got in little groups and talked. Maybe we were planning our next strategy for the upcoming softball game, or maybe we were trying to talk the teacher into an extended recess for the next time we got to go outside. Some even gathered around the piano and sang some songs. Even on those days when Ole Man Weather got in our way, we had fun! I am a believer that school should be fun, and that includes both play and learning.

Annie Over

Annie Over is a most fun game. It is played as sort of another form of dodgeball, but with a very strong element of honor and trust involved. Have you noticed how all of these games I am writing about teach something? Math, honesty, integrity, toughness, respect, trust, physical growth, fairness, winning, losing, getting along, and so on—these are all virtues that transcend politics and religion. In Annie Over, we simply chose sides, and one team got on each side of the school building. We usually played with two balls. To begin the game, team 1 would throw the balls over the building right after shouting, "Annie Over!" By the way, getting the balls over the building wasn't all that easy.

The rules were clear. Before you threw, you had to announce it. Thus, "Annie Over" was announced. If, as a receiving team, we caught the balls, we were allowed to charge around the building in either direction. Upon arriving, we could throw the balls at our opponents. If someone was hit, that player or players were out of the game. The receiving team was on their honor as to the catching of the balls. It seemed to work pretty well back then. I am not sure it would fly today, in the win-at-all-costs environment we seem to live in.

Our strategy was usually to charge from both ends. We were good at hiding the balls and making our opponents have a hard time figuring out who had them. Often it was possible to get more than one player out by getting in a couple of throws before they could escape around the building to the side we had just vacated. At that point, the Annie Over was relinquished to the team that had just finished being the receiver, and now it was their turn to yell, "Annie Over," throw the balls over the building, and wait for the charge around the building so the other team could even up the score.

And so the game continued, until one team or the other ran out of players. I will confess that it was normal for a player, once he or she had been eliminated from the game, to monitor the other team, just to be sure the honor system was established and being practiced. Another little strategy we came up with was to, instead of throwing the caught balls, hold on to them and tag as many of the other team as we could before they escaped to the other side. At that point, we would take one last desperation throw and maybe get one more out. The first time we did this, as I recall, the other team challenged this strategy, and so it wound up in arbitration, with the teacher being the arbitrator. She ruled that is sounded to her like a fair and improved strategy to make the game an even better game than it already was. So it became an improved and genuine rule of

Annie Over at Scotland Elementary School. As for me, I enjoyed throwing more than I did tagging. It was fun!

Football

I love the game of football. I've been a part of it my whole life; it was even my chosen vocation at one point. I wish I could say my one-room country school pointed me in that direction. Actually it was my dad who pointed me toward football. I ended up coaching it. Both our boys played it, and one went on to play and coach at the collegiate level. All of us learned a lot about life from our days on the football field. But nonetheless, we did have a football at Scotland Elementary School. I suspect my dad made sure of that. He played the game back in the day at Pierce City High School in Missouri, and he truly loved the experience. He would have been a great coach.

But in a one-room country school, what can you do with a football? We had no coaches, no organized physical education classes, and no television that showed us how to play—or should I say how *not* to play. So we created our own version of football. Actually, I am confident this version had already been invented, but somehow we got hold of it and made it fit our circumstances. I am sure you know the game I speak of. It is commonly called kick over. It is, still today, a very popular game. One team punts to their opponent, and they try to catch the ball before it hits the ground. If they do, they are allowed to take ten giant steps forward and punt it back. I use the word "punt" because there is a difference between a punt and a kick. (In the words of my teacher, "Look it up. You'll learn more.") And so the process of punting and catching goes back and forth between the two teams until one team punts it over the other team's goal line without it being caught.

Remember: I told you I went to Duenweg Elementary in the third grade. That is where I learned to play kick over football. I am not taking credit for introducing it to Scotland, but there is a chance I did. For eight years of grade school, this was my exposure to the game of football. I will admit, though, that my dad and I did play some in the backyard.

My reason for going to college was to become a football coach. I figured this out during my high school playing days at Carterville High School in Carterville, Missouri. I was the first in my family to attend college, and I am very proud that both of my brothers followed suit and went on to earn college degrees. I am equally proud that both of our boys went on to participate in college athletics and that one of them professionally coached. I have often told people that the best three things I have ever been called are "husband," "Dad," and "Coach." I have revised that list to rethink this some, and so these days I say, "husband, Dad, Paw Paw, and Coach." And I have to say that "Paw Paw" is in a dead heat with "husband" and "Dad" for first place.

Softball

We were a softball school. Yep, other than a county spelling bee that took place once a year, it was our only interschool activity. We actually did compete against other one-room country schools in our area. I must say that it was a tough league. It definitely was, and still is today, a game of strategy. Of course, the strategy we employed was much different from what you would witness in today's games. But nonetheless, it was strategy. It was normal that every team had a very good player or two and also would have some that I'll just say were very young and inexperienced. When a good hitter for one of the teams would come up to bat, the team in the field would move their players around to spots they figured the ball was most likely to be hit to. Today they call this a shift. Professional baseball teams are just now figuring this out. Shoot, we were doing this back in the day. But I am not talking about a left fielder playing closer to the line because the batter is a pull hitter, or a shortstop playing on the first-base side of second base because the batter is left handed. No, I am talking about a shortstop who would move all the way out to left field, knowing the batter would most likely hit it hard and in the air to left field. We all knew each other, and it worked.

A dad, if we were lucky—and sometimes two dads, if we were very lucky—would umpire the game. After the game, we would all eat watermelon, win or lose. I don't remember too much about the wins or losses, but I do remember, to this day, the name of the player from the other school we had to adjust to. He attended Scotland Elementary School with me for a while but moved to the community of Atlas, where he attended Underwood, their one-room country school. When that happened, even though we were good friends, we competed hard against each other. We went on to be best friends at Carterville High. His name was John Gaddis. His brother Jerry and his sister Patty also played. Both John and I played shortstop for our respective teams, and both of us, when the other was batting, moved out to deep left field. That is no brag, just a fact. What good memories. The watermelon was the best part. Fun, fun!

One other little addition to this story is the time I umpired a softball game at Perseverance Elementary School. It was another one-room country school not far from Scotland that I had competed against when I attended Scotland. The teacher who invited me to come umpire a game was Lou Jamison, one of my former teachers at Scotland. I really don't know how I did that day, but I do know I learned that it is not an easy job and so my respect for umpires grew some. Anyway, it was a good experience, and I was proud to do it. A side note is that Perseverance was the elementary school my future wife attended. She too cherishes those one-room country school days.

12

THE LONG RECESS: OUR TEACHER'S VERY SERIOUS INJURY

This seems like an appropriate time to insert this story. It has to do with our practicing for a softball game and our teacher's involvement. It's sad, but yet it is a story of a teacher doing what had to be done—and doing it with class. As I have already said, she was and is an angel.

Our softball field was on the north side of the school. It was the only nearly level spot we had. The prairie sloped from west to east, and even on our somewhat level playing field, the right fielder was playing on a hill and looking up toward the infield. Often, our teacher would stand in the doorway located in the northeast corner of the building and actually umpire our games. Yep, she was a good fifty feet or so from home plate, but we never argued her calls. In fact, I don't believe she ever got one wrong. If you stop to think about it, we have fans today that argue with the umpire on his calls from three hundred feet away. The bottom line was that in our games, there were no arguments. She saw it all! Of course, she wasn't always able to ump for us; and on those occasions, we called our own games. Again, there were no arguments.

On one particular day in the spring of my eighth-grade year, in preparation for an upcoming softball game with another school, we were having a good practice. We were playing our biggest rival, Underwood Elementary. Underwood was the school that housed the Atlas community students as well as those from other outlying areas, much as Scotland did. Atlas was the home of Atlas Powder and provided many jobs in the area. At that point in our history, we were evidently not educated as to the environmental damages caused by this company's chemical waste. It was evident in the plant life, and especially the trees, that it was having a detrimental effect on the surrounding area. And I am positive the air we breathed was less than safe. Environmental protection laws were not yet in full force, and even if they had been, the economic impact this company had on the area by providing much-needed jobs was immeasurable. Anyway, that is another story for another time.

Back to my softball game and its story. Recess was about to come to an end. The wind had picked up drastically, as it often does on the prairie. I remember glancing over toward our teacher, Lou Jamison. She was standing in the open doorway, and I could tell she was about to ring the bell. During that split second, I witnessed the heavy steel door blow shut. I didn't think too much about it, because she had taught us that if she wasn't available, we were to go right ahead and make the calls on our own. So our practice continued. I knew the recess had gone over the allotted time she had granted us. Often she would let it extend on purpose if she happened to be busy with a student or maybe as a reward for our behavior in school. But as five minutes extra grew into maybe fifteen minutes extra, I made the decision to go check. I thought perhaps she had forgotten to ring the bell, but that sure didn't seem likely.

I opened the door, and there she was. She was lying on her back on the floor, positioned between two rows of desks. The force of the door hitting her had knocked her back into the room several feet. She immediately motioned for me to come to her. I was really, really scared. I could tell she was badly hurt. She said, "Raymond, be brave. It will be okay. Listen to me." Then she spelled out for me exactly what I was to do. Her instructions were clear, and I remember them, like it happened yesterday.

1. "Go get another boy to help."
2. "Don't tell anyone."
3. "The two of you come back and help me get in my chair."

I did as she said. We returned, and I am sorry, but I really don't remember who helped me. It must have been a seventh grader because the other two eighth graders were both girls. Upon our arrival, she instructed us to get her chair from behind her desk. (It did not have casters.) We did as instructed. She placed one of us on each side of her head. She proceeded to explain to us where we should lift and how to use our legs and not our backs in the process. She was a large woman, and to this day I have no idea how we managed to get her into her chair, but we did. It surely was an unbearable pain she endured during this happening, but she never once let out a peep. I am confident she must have done most of the work in order for us to have accomplished this task.

Of course we didn't know it at the time, but she had suffered a severely broken hip. Again, the pain she must have felt as we scooted her chair from the very back of the room all the way to the front of the room had to be excruciating. Upon arriving, we scooted her to a position where she would be sitting behind her desk. Once we got her behind her desk, it appeared to at least give her some support. She had the arms of the chair on each side of her and her large desk in front of her.

We were to tell none of the students of the accident. She told us to ring the bell for the kids to come in from recess. "Raymond, as soon as they are all in and roll has been taken, you quietly slip out the back door. Run as fast as you can to your home." She knew my mother would be there. She went on to say, "Tell her to get help and to hurry." And then she added, "Don't tell anyone what has happened except your mother. She will know what to do."

I should explain the above quotes. These are the words I remember. They may not be her exact words. But I quoted them because you have my assurance that they represent exactly what I was told to do. She knew my mom would be at home and would have the car because she had driven the neighborhood to school that same morning. It was sort of an unwritten caution among the community that whoever drove the kids to school on a given day would stay close to home in case there was a need at school. There were no phones. All she had to get her the help she needed was a scared eighth grader—and one that was not a very fast runner on top of that. Even if Mom had not had the car on that day, she would have soon rounded one up and taken care of the problem. Ms. Jamison knew that was the case when she told me, "Go tell your mother."

I can't remember that run. I can't say I ran fast all the way, but I can say I ran hard all the way. Fast for a Dykens, at this time, would receive a grade of C at best. I remember that my fear left me as I ran. I was simply doing what my teacher told me to do, and I sure didn't want to let her down. I somehow realized the importance of my mission and that she was depending on me to get it done. My heart was pounding as I burst through the front door of my house. I am sure I shouted and did the best I could to inform my mom of the situation. I don't remember her immediate reaction, but I am positive she hugged me and calmed me down. I imagine she may have said, "Talk slowly and tell me exactly what Ms. Jamison said."

Soon Mom had rounded up some help and we were headed back to the school. I really don't remember who the help was. It could have been any of a number of people. I just knew that help was on its way. I suspect there were several community members not far behind as we arrived back at the school. Soon our teacher was on her way to the hospital, and I remember that those who came to help made sure that all the kids got home safely. And I will testify in court to the following being true: As Mom and I and others arrived to help our teacher, she was sitting at her desk and conducting school as if nothing had ever happened. I seriously doubt that any of the kids other than I and the boy who helped me get her in the chair ever suspected a thing until that moment.

I am sad to say that Ms. Jamison was not able to finish the school year as our teacher. Others filled in for the short term. When these types of situations occurred, it was not uncommon for members of the community to fill in and do the teaching until a certified replacement could be found. I do know there were times this happened at Scotland, and I am even aware that my dad was one who filled in at one point. That happened after I had already graduated, but my brothers were still at Scotland. I remember my brother Jim being so proud of his dad filling in and doing such a great job. This doesn't surprise me, because his mother was also a teacher in a one-room country school.

On this occasion, though, at least as I recall, it was Lou Jamison's sister who filled in. She had been a teacher, and it was a good temporary fit because it allowed us to be in daily communication with our teacher. As I remember, this worked out as best it could under the circumstances and allowed us to continue having school until a certified replacement could be found. I am not sure of the time it took, but the district was able to bring back Zoe Wommack to finish our year. Ms. Wommack knew the school and community well, and we were blessed to be able to secure her services. Through Ms. Jameson's sister, we were able to keep in touch with her. I remember Mom taking me to see her a few times during her recovery. Today I say, "Thank You, God, for Your divine intervention in all our lives on that day. With Your guidance, we made it. Amen!" My grandmother Dykens was a teacher in a one-room country school, and I can imagine she would have been this type of teacher. The following picture is of her and her students at Hill Side DIC Country No. 62 in 1905.

MORE ACTIVITIES

Stilt Walk

It was a ritual each year that we could make our own stilts and have a stilt day at school. We had races and contests of all kinds, and we took a lot of pride in who could stay up the longest on the highest pair of stilts. I won one year because I had the tallest stilts. My stilts were so high that I had to climb on top of the boys' outhouse to get on them. They were so tall they bent when I walked on them. Everyone was so impressed, and this time it didn't even cost me a trip to the dentist. I wish I had been able to take a picture. I don't remember how far or how long I stayed up, but I would venture to say that it was at least a distance of a first and ten. That would be thirty feet for all you non–football fans. I doubt it took very long to cover that distance, because once I got them going, it was difficult to slow down and impossible to stop. I was so proud!

Snowball Fights and Snow Forts

There isn't much I can say about snowball fights and snow forts. They go together. A snowball fight then is the same as a snowball fight now. We had to have a couple of rules. Just as with knock-down-and-drag-out, participants were allowed to opt out of these. Secondly, we had a rule that we could not "pack them tight." I'm sure we all obeyed that one. We didn't break the rule, but we did, shall I say, squeeze the rule a bit. Of course, forts were built, attacks were launched, and defenses were tested. Preparing for the fight was as much fun as the fight itself. It was considered a big kids' game, but anyone was allowed to play. In addition to the above-mentioned rules, it was also agreed on that there was to be "no crying." I know it sounds bad, but honestly the big kids were very careful with the little ones. I really don't remember many tears. Much of the credit for this, I'm sure, can be given to the very professionally designed forts we constructed. The fact is that a good time was had by all.

Ice-Skating

In a nearby pasture was a shallow pond we often used for skating. To be sure it would hold up, it was necessary to test it. This had to be done before we allowed it to be used as a skating rink. Here I go again with another true story. As an eighth grader, testing the ice was my job. It was my eighth-grade year, and I was the "official ice pond, skating maybe, checker-outer." I remember sliding across one day as the ice was cracking behind me. Of course, it was not cracking all the way through. I returned to the school and reported my scientific observation to the teacher. It went something like this: "The ice has a few minor cracks in it, but it should hold up fine." She never bought it, and so there was no skating that day. The kids were all mad at me, and I remember being mad at her for not trusting my judgment. I never told my mom that story. I have a feeling that she and the teacher would have had a little chitchat.

Sleigh Rides

Each year, Shorty Baker would bring his tractor to school with a big homemade sleigh behind it. He would give us all rides across the prairie. His son, David, was a grade ahead of me and went on to be a teacher of mathematics at the collegiate level. The last I knew, which was in 2012, he and his wife owned a flower shop in Joplin, Missouri. To the best of my knowledge, they still do.

I remember the Baker family as being a very musically talented family. They were smart, hard workers, churchgoing people and great supporters of our school and community. Anyway, these sleigh rides were fun, and after each one, hot chocolate would be waiting for us at the schoolhouse. I suspect Shorty's wife had a lot to do with this, along with David's sister Mary. Yep, Shorty was a good guy, and as I am sure you can guess, he loved kids.

Camel Fights (Busted Heinie)

This was a simple game but probably not a game we should have been playing. Maybe a better version would have been more suitable for our age group, or maybe I just have sour grapes because of my nearly serious injury. Many of you will recognize the game from your experience of playing it in the swimming pool. That is the version I would recommend. The game, as we played it on the playground at Scotland Elementary School, began with pairing up some bigger boys with some smaller boys. Age sort of mattered, but not as much as aggressiveness. The smaller boy would sit on the shoulders of the bigger and stronger boy. We played the game where each pair took on all comers, and we also played using teams, with the same number of pairs on each team. The object of the game was to maneuver in such a way as to knock the other pair to the ground. To score, one had to, at least, knock off an opposing rider. The only problem with knocking off just the rider was that he could remount, and he and his partner could reenter the game. If you were able to knock both to the ground and at least one knee of the base partner touched the ground, you not only scored two points (one for each boy down), but both opposing players were out of the game and neither could reenter. I don't recall any other rules. When playing in teams, much like knock-down-and-drag-out, a team could gang up on one pair and remove them from the game early. If it was every pair for themselves, the pairs simply kept track of the points they earned. There we go again with the honor system. You know what? It worked! Would it work today? I leave you to answer that. I would like to think that it would.

As for the busted heinie part of this story, it went like this. It was an injury I received during my participation in this game. I was a rider when I was maybe a fifth grader or perhaps a sixth grader. I was really hit hard one day, knocking me from the shoulders of my teammate and to the ground. I hit squarely on my tailbone. I still believe, to this day, that I broke it. I never told anyone—not even my parents. But I should have. I didn't want to get others in trouble or perhaps even have the game declared over and done with forever. Again, I still should have told someone. I was lucky, and I admit I didn't play the game much after that—at least until I was old enough and strong enough to be the carrier. I have to say the game was a lot of fun. But I have to also say you should keep the game confined to the swimming pool.

Grass Tunnels

As I have mentioned several times, our school's setting was a beautiful prairie. So we had lots of prairie grass to play with. During a certain time of the year, it became brittle and easy to pull. We would gather it in bunches and spend many, many recesses and many, many days shaping these bunches of prairie grass into tunnels. They were all connected and spread over a great portion of the playground. One rule we had was that we had to build them on the "window side" of the school. Now, I wonder why? Because of their brittleness, they were actually fairly sturdy, and depending on the weather, they would last several days. We worked hard building these tunnels, and the little kids sure had a great time crawling through them. Our teacher must have loved these days, as we were all pretty much involved in the same project. Anyone who decided to tear them up was in some big-time peer trouble.

I know you must be wondering about the bugs, spiders, snakes, mice, skunks, and the like. If they were there, I never knew it. I just know it was a fun project to make this maze of straw tunnels and that a great time was had by all. I wish I had a picture to share with you, but of course my smartphone was dead on the day we made all these tunnels. Okay, that's not the truth, but you get my point. I hope you can use your imagination and picture, along with me, a great time during which we all worked together to make it happen. What a concept! Perhaps our world should revisit this line of thinking a bit. Okay, I'll move on before I get way too far from my playground—or at least that's what it was as I remember it.

*****

All we did was play, right? I know it is beginning to sound like that way. But that would be far from the truth. Needless to say, there were other games we invented as we went along, and some I probably should not write about. Those I have forgotten; I promise. The ones I have written about are most memorable to me and everyone played them often. Board games, red rover, all forms of tag, post office, and spin the bottle are among a few games I did not cover. (I would have written about post office, but I have no real experience with it. I only observed it from a distance because I was a full-fledged member of the local "women haters club." Please, ladies, don't be offended. It was an early-grade stage I went through, and I assure you I soon reevaluated my stance on that subject.)

I admit we played our games with a certain amount of orneriness involved at times. Were we sometimes rude and ill-mannered in our play? Sure! Were we always friendly and never in trouble? Nope! We were kids, but I will be quick to say that the fights were few and far between. And from those experiences, we did learn about respect for each other. We were usually our own officials. We never saw or heard of the misuse of tobacco on the school grounds except for the one story recorded earlier about the pipe-smoking first grader. We knew drugs were in a cabinet at home and were never to be touched without the guidance of Mom or Dad. Alcohol was never mentioned, at least at school. On rare occasions, one might hear the uttering of a curse word. Even with that being the case, I didn't know the *F* word even existed until I entered high school. I am very proud to have retired as a public school educator. But I must say that the playgrounds of today do not meet the above described standard. But please, do not be discouraged. We are working on it, and our young people are responding favorably. If I had been faced with what they are faced with today, I am sure my testimony would be much different. I believe our future is in good hands and our youth of today will make us proud.

Cheating was not a problem, because the rest of the kids would never have allowed it. Playing fair was important. Third graders played with eighth graders, and it worked. Eighth graders took care of me when I was in the lower grades, and when I was an eighth grader, I took care of the kids in the lower grades. I'm sorry, but I don't often enough see this kind of watch in today's world. I am in no way suggesting we return to the one-room country school, but I am saying we need to do a better job of protecting our little ones from the dangers that surround them. I am very proud to be a product of the one-room country school and what it taught me. But I am equally proud to have been a part of the growth in public education in this country for over forty years. The opportunities afforded our young people in the schoolrooms of today are immeasurable.

We never had to face the same pressures our young people face today. It is tough being young, and it will take every one of us to keep this country strong with high standards that protect and ensure everyone a free and safe environment in which to learn. We have good schools, good parents, and great kids. Hang in there; our future is in good hands. Every school I was privileged to be a part of worked hard at teaching kids, not subjects. Both are important, but remember that the worth of an individual far outweighs the most complicated math formula. These are my opinions. The key to our future lies in a standard that has always been true. It was true in the one-room country school, and it's true now: we must treat others the way we wish to be treated.

SHOWTIME

Land Ho!

School plays were huge! We did at least three or four a year with all the trimmings. I was honored to be cast as several different characters over the years. I've portrayed everyone from Columbus to Simple Simon. Okay, I am about to humble myself big time as I share with you a true story. It was the one where I played Columbus on his way to discover America. As with all plays, we had to be in costume. As Simple Simon, I wore a pair of pink pants and a short pink jacket. (I never cared much for this particular costume.) Our moms were responsible for the making of all costumes. My mom usually wound up making not only mine but several others as well. She was a very good seamstress, and of course she did it for nothing. So she had lots of opportunities to volunteer.

I return now to my true story of my portrayal of Columbus. Allow me to set the stage as I prepare, even now as I did then, to embarrass myself. Please understand I was just a little guy, perhaps in the fifth or sixth grade. The scene I wish to expound on was the one where the three ships under the leadership of Columbus were getting close to their destination. The ships were the Niña, Pinta, and Santa Maria, and they were crossing the ocean, looking for a new land. For the ships, we used washtubs. When I say "washtubs," I really mean bathtubs—the kind that we carried hot water to when it was bath time. We carried the water from the coal or wood stove, the only source of heat in our house. And yes, when my family first moved to Scotland, we had a coal-burning stove, a wood stove in the kitchen, and an outhouse. We did have one large bathtub. It usually sat behind the stove that was the source of the heat for its water. This at least made the trip to the tub with the hot water a little shorter. Such tubs were often found in the kitchen or the living room. A few of you readers have perhaps had this experience. If so, I am confident you will testify that the tubs were not very comfortable and that unless you got to go first, the whole deal was not very pleasant.

Okay, back to my story. Anyway, for our play about Columbus, we had one long tub and two round ones. The round ones were classified as single-occupancy tubs, although it was possible for a couple of kids to share one. For the main ship on our voyage across the sea, we had a long oblong one. Perfect! It would hold two or even three kids but still was classified as a single-occupancy tub for adults. An oblong tub was sure enough considered a luxury item in one's home; with one of these, an adult could actually finally enjoy the experience of bathing while being able to stretch out his or her legs.

Our main ship in our play, the oblong one, had at its helm none other than Christopher Columbus himself. That would be me. I was so proud I had earned that role. My crew was behind me. There were two in the large tub with me, and one each in the two round tubs. I wish I could remember who it was that held those spots. I know I made them all proud that day. There we were, sailing the ocean blue. Did I mention that I was the star in this production? I was well aware that I had been given my lines, as had the others. Along with these lines came the instructions to learn them. A dress rehearsal practice was scheduled the next day. I think I remember reading my lines, but I'm not sure. Regardless, I do remember practice the next day. What I remember is that I was trying to fake it. I had no clue what my lines were. I was doing the best I could and seemed to be handling the situation just like a movie star would.

The tubs were in place; mine was the tub in front (ship, I mean). Since we had only had our parts for a day or so, we were allowed to have them in our hands for the practice. I was reading ahead and masterfully spouting out my lines as they came due. I was proud I was doing this without reading from the script. Pretty impressive, wouldn't you say? The scene I am about to describe is the one where Columbus sights land.

Yep, the teacher said, "Okay, everyone, lay down your scripts, and let's get the acting part correct. Columbus, you stand in the front of your ship, put one foot upon the edge, lean forward with your hand over your forehead as if you are looking as far out as you can see, and then cry out!" That was all she said—"Cry out!" I had no clue what I was supposed to say or do. She was so insistent, and she became more and more impatient with me. "Columbus, cry out!" So I did! This was my very best of efforts ever. With all the volume and energy I could muster, I let it go. It was the very loudest, shrill, and most convincing cry ever uttered. It wasn't a whine, and it was much more than a baby's cry. It was a very, very good cry! Some of my classmates screamed, probably because they were so proud of me. Some laughed, probably because they thought it was all part of the act. Most of them just stared in disbelief. Like me, they probably had not read the script. I never heard the teacher shouting at me to stop. I finally did, but only after I had run out of breath and completely exhausted my lungs. I admit that I was most happy to see that my teacher was joining in with the ones laughing. Actually, come to think of it, she was laughing louder than anyone, and had it not been rude, I am convinced she would have been on the floor rolling. I was so relieved! I knew I had performed well. After all, as with most of our productions, it was sort of a comedy, and it was sure enough getting a good laugh.

To this day, I really believe she gave strong consideration to leaving it in the play exactly as I had done it. But of course she didn't. She simply coached me up and explained that I was to cry out "Land ho!" It's tough being an actor.

On this day, I went from the front of the tub to the rear of the tub in the snap of a finger. From then on, I read ahead and asked questions. For example, even though I did not have my script in front of me when she asked me to cry out, I should have asked her to demonstrate for me so I would be sure to get it right. Instead, I panicked. Oh well, it turned out okay. I earned my way back to the front of the tub. I still got to play Columbus, the play went great, Mom and Dad were proud, and I made my teacher laugh. I hope that's good, because at age seventy-five, I am big-time embarrassed and have, until now, shared this story with very few people. Forgive me, but it is the truth! Read on; I have more.

Of course, we performed several plays, and they were always well attended by the community. Looking back on them, I have to say they were among our very best teaching aids. We learned structure, discipline, history, teamwork, hard work, sacrifice, give-and-take, memorization, research, success, failure, motivation, self-discipline, and the feeling of having done a good job. Are these not a few of the lessons in life that we all should be working on to some degree? I'll leave it at that, along with my pictures of my fleet of ships and the entire crew.

*****

Now, you might think this must have been the most embarrassing moment of my elementary school days, and perhaps it was. But there were others, and the one running a close second to this one happened at a pie and box supper. These also would have to be labeled as events that were indeed showtime happenings. I once believed that everyone knew what these were. Now I know better. For those that may not know, allow me to explain. The girls would all bring a pie-or-box supper to the school on an evening designated for this community affair. The box would contain a meal for two. The boxes and pies were auctioned to raise money for the school. The boxes were decorated and did not identify their makers. (Of course, there were ways of finding out.) The idea was for a boy or man to buy a box and hope it belonged to the one he wanted to eat with. The adults did most of the bidding, buying, and eating. In fact, most of the time it was Dad who bought Mom's box. It always contained enough for us boys. But we eighth graders wanted to do our own thing. (That part of being an eighth grader hasn't changed much over the years.) Of course, we had no money. So here comes another true story.

I Had to Eat with a Girl

During one of these events, my dad bought a box in my name. Somehow he knew it had been made by a girl I liked. (I told you I would get over that woman-hater thing.) At least I thought I liked her. Sure enough, we sat together at a desk made for one, and we even had a few bites. I learned very quickly that I was not the one she had hoped would buy the box. I also was very aware that everyone was staring at us. This was not fun! We were, however, polite to each other. Even though we were sitting close together, it was a short and very distant meal.

This experience ended my desire to eat with a girl at one of these happenings. Never again would I do that. Since then, I have purchased pies made by my wife a few times. These did not come cheap. We took them home and enjoyed them in front of a Saint Louis Cardinals baseball game. Now *that* was fun! Really, though, these were great community gatherings. There was always some special music provided by local musicians, student presentations, and lots of visiting. In short, it was good, clean family fun. These types of experiences are getting harder and harder to find, are they not? I'll share with you in other chapters more about some of these programs. For now I'll just say that the box supper described above was a little embarrassing. However, it remains a fond childhood memory—not because I got to eat with a girl, but rather because my dad was having some fun with me and trying to please me. No, I didn't grow up and marry this girl, but I did marry one who was attending a one-room country school not too far away from Scotland. I didn't know her at the time, but I am so thankful I found her. Or did she find me? Anyway, I am betting somewhere along the way she probably had a box lunch with someone she really didn't want to eat with. Regardless, if she did, he was a very lucky young man because my wife can flat out cook.

That Doggie in the Window

From school plays and pie-and-box suppers to musical performances, we pretty much kept this little school hopping with some great performances. My favorite musical performance story is special to me because it was my first public solo, and yes, I fell in love with singing and performing in front of an audience. Some of you, I am sure, will remember the song "How Much Is That Doggie in the Window?"

I've always enjoyed performing in front of people and especially on stage. I am in no way saying I am good at it. But I did and still do enjoy doing it. I had an uncle who played the guitar and sang country songs for community gatherings in and around Pierce City, Missouri. His name is Morris Palmer, and he is one of my mother's brothers. She had four others, and they were all gifted in art, music, or both. One of them, Uncle Hubert, was a designer for Hallmark Cards. A side note here is that he had the honor of engraving the Christmas card used by President Carter and Vice President Mondale. On my father's side, several of my cousins—Lewis, Doyle, and Dale—and my aunt Eva were all gifted in this respect. As I recall, some of them even had their own early-morning radio show. Anyway, my point is that the family on both sides had genes rich with musical talent. While I may have received a smattering of them, I was very average at music and had zero patience for art.

However, determined to sing a solo at one of our school programs, I asked Uncle Morris if he would play the guitar for me while I sang. He said he would be honored. We decided on the song "How Much Is That Doggie in the Window?" I am very sure it was the accompaniment that held it together the night I sang my song. But you know what? I believe I did a good job. That is what Uncle Morris told me, and so it must be true. Thanks to him and my mom, I learned enough to play and sing a little the rest of my life. Of course, my efforts were just for fun, but nonetheless, it became a tradition that was passed on to my two sons, Alan and Andy. And today, they are passing it along to my grandchildren,

Dixie, Bode, Sevi, and Ellie. By the way, they all are very talented. I don't remember if we got a standing ovation that night or not, but I will tell you that if we didn't, we should have. And that is the way I remember it.

Yellow Rose of Texas

For this number, I believe I was in the seventh grade. I must have been, because David Baker was the piano player, and he was an eighth grader. I was on the guitar. If he were telling you the story, he would probably tell you that it was his song and I was his accompaniment. And he sort of would be telling you the truth. The title of the song was "The Yellow Rose of Texas." After our performance, David accused me of never changing chords on my guitar. He was right. It was a fast song, and I didn't have time because I couldn't change that fast. I just stayed fixed on the C chord while he threw in the G7, an F, and a minor or two. I figured that if I stayed right there in C, he would soon be back, and that was when I would play louder. It worked—at least as far as I am concerned. Hey, my parents had the same smiles on their faces as David's parents did. At least I think they did. It was all good, and it was fun!

Bimbo

This performance was a vocal duet with my brother Jim. Well, I sort of goofed this one up too. Since I am five years older than Jim, I believe I must have been a seventh grader. I just knew the seventh grade was my time to shine. Jim may have been a third grader. We were to sing that famous piece "Bimbo." You know the one: "Bimbo, Bimbo, where are you gonna go-e-o." We were all set to go until we got ready to actually start the song. There was no piano and no guitar this time, just our beautiful voices. It was my job to get us started on the right key. I could not do it! For the sake of me, I could not get the song started. No matter what I tried, I failed. I kept trying, beginning again and again. "Bimbo ... Bimbo ... Bimbo."

I knew that was the first word in the song, and I tried every pitch and key as I tried to muster up the tune. Finally, a girl offstage in the cloak room got us started. Her name was Patty Gaddis. Thank you, Patty.

Once we got started, Jim and I did fine. In fact, I thought we did great. But Jim had other notions about his future as a singer. Jim never sang with me, or for that matter anyone, ever again. I believe that to be a true statement. I may be wrong, but I doubt it. Now, he has performed on stage a time or two with his mandolin, and I'm told he did great. On one occasion years later, after he had become an elementary school principal, he did a lip-sync impersonation of Elvis Presley, I believe. I didn't see it in person, but I did see a video of it. I couldn't believe it. It was a truly great performance. But again, it was kind of a karaoke deal. He never actually sang. Jim, I am so sorry. I know you would be sharing time on stage with Waylon, Willie, and the boys if it had not been for "Bimbo" and me. Anyway, Jim is smarter than I am. I am still trying to sing some, and most of the time I can get the song started, but not every time.

Mom in a Minstrel

I hesitated to write this story, but it is part of my experience as a young lad who didn't know any better. Minstrel shows were very common productions in those days. We lived in an area of the country where there were few people of color. I speak specifically of African Americans. In my home, they were referred to as colored folks or Negroes. To my knowledge, there were none in Scotland, Duenweg, Atlas, or Prosperity. These were my neighboring communities. I know for sure there were none in the elementary schools of these particular communities. At least, in my travels to the communities, I never saw any. When we would travel to Joplin for groceries, we might see one or two. But even on these occasions, we did not see them often. I remember I was a little afraid of them. Please understand that my parents never taught me to be afraid of them. In fact, my mother taught me to respect all people of all colors; as she said, "They are all God's children." And so the following story seems a little strange that I would include it, because of my mother's teachings. Later in life, she would have no part in telling or hearing about the time she participated in a "Negro minstrel." She was truly ashamed she had done that. But again, in those days, it was a most common form of entertainment.

The show was a Scotland community production and was held at the Scotland schoolhouse. Participants who could sing painted their faces black. Their attire covered all other white skin. They put on what might be described as a musical. My mom could flat out sing, and so she was highly recruited for this production. I am sure the production included some Negro spirituals and some folk songs. I am equally confident it was well done. It was not a production that intended to make fun of or be negative to the Negro race. Of course, this was from the perspective of white people. I am confident they, as a minimum, saw it as an attempt to imitate them—and a poor one at that. (I should point out also that it was not uncommon for Negro entertainers to perform in these shows as well.) Nevertheless, it was a success and went over very well as a good evening of entertainment for the community of Scotland.

I remember, as a young adult, bringing this happening up for discussion with Mom. She quickly made it clear that she should never have done it and that it was not to be brought up again. As time went on, I tried to convince her that it had occurred at a time in our society when it was not only acceptable but also in demand. I probably even said something stupid like "It's okay, Mom; you didn't know any better." I must also confess that at the time of its showing, I never realized, in any way, that it might not be a good thing to do. I was only thrilled that my mom participated and that she performed on stage and sang to an audience. I was so proud of her. Mom, if you are looking upon this writing and the telling of this story, please forgive me. It's just that I feel it to be an important part of our history that I hope we learned from. Perhaps some of you may recall the days when such Negro minstrel names as Al Jolsen and Billy Van were considered stars in "blackface productions." Even Bugs Bunny appeared in blackface in 1953. Are there prejudices in our world today? Oh my, yes! But have we, in America, at least to some degree, begun to believe that we are all God's children? To some degree we have, but in my opinion, we sure have a ways to go.

VETERANS DAY: A TEARFUL EXPERIENCE

I have already introduced my father to you as a WWII Veteran. I was probably in the fifth or sixth grade when my dad was invited to the school on Veterans Day. He was asked to talk with us about veterans and what it means to be one. As a recipient of the Silver Star for heroics during the Normandy Invasion on Omaha Beach and the Bronze Star for gallantry under enemy fire during a battle in Germany, he was a perfect candidate to represent all veterans. At least, this was how my teacher figured it after I had made sure she knew of his WWII involvement. And so I was delegated to ask him if he would come to our school, in uniform, and give us a talk about our freedoms and what soldiers do to help us keep those freedoms.

What could he say? I had no idea at that time how hard that would be for him. I don't mean speaking in front of people. After all, he stayed in the Army Reserve following the war and retired as a command sergeant major. You do not rise to that rank by being silent. But this was different. If I had known then what I learned later in life, I would never have asked him to do that. It was very selfish on my part. My dad, in uniform, would make a speech to all of us. It was, in my opinion, the envy of the school. And as promised, he came. He stood before us and told us, with pride, of our freedoms. He told how many had died so that we could be "free." He told us how proud he and all veterans were to have served. He went on to say that we should, whenever we meet a veteran, say, "Thank you." He told us that a thank-you was all they expected or wanted. "Just a thank-you."

He was doing well until he asked if anyone had any questions. Looking back on that day, I can remember the look he got on his face as he began to reflect. His mind turned to his buddies and their experiences—experiences best left in the back of one's mind. I don't believe it was a question that caused a flashback. I just feel he went back into his mind without intending to. Then it happened! I've seen my dad break down and cry a very few times in his life. I remember it happening once at a movie where Bing Crosby and Bob Hope were entertaining the troops in Europe during WWII. And it happened again at the funerals of some very close family members. But this day is recorded now as one of those very few times. He tried to recover but just couldn't. He turned and walked outside as we all silently watched. Our teacher quickly took over and explained what had just happened. I am sure she did a great job. She motioned to me that I should go outside and see my dad.

As I approached him, he pulled himself together. I didn't know what to say. He looked down with tears in his eyes and apologized to me. I have no idea of my response. But even at my age, I was very sure he owed no one, especially me, an apology. I've always hoped he saw that in my face as I stood silently encircled in his embrace. I learned, on this day, just a tiny bit about war and what it does to one. I recognized a veteran who was full of some very sad and awful memories, along with a special love for his buddies—and theirs for him.

Years later, I visited the Korean War Veterans Memorial in Washington, DC. The inscription on the wall by that memorial reads, "The Price of Freedom is Not Free." I close this writing by saying to my dad what I should have said on that day: "Dad, I could not be more proud of you." In his honor, I retired after thirty-two years of service in the Army National Guard. I was fortunate in that I never saw combat. I am proud of my service, but as a soldier, I couldn't carry my dad's duffel bag. Thank you, Dad!

The following writings are excerpts from a letter submitted by Jerry Endicott. Jerry's family lived right across the street from me and my family, and they too were part of a village that worked together to take care of our school and community. In his letter, he says, "As I think back, I find it amazing that one teacher was in charge of teaching and controlling eight grades in a one-room schoolhouse." He and his brother Ron were janitors one year, and like me, they found it to be a rewarding and valuable experience. I am especially grateful for Jerry's remembrance of my dad. He wrote in his letter the following: "One day, Charles Dykens, Raymond's dad, came to our school dressed in his US Army uniform. He gave us a talk about his experiences in World War II." Jerry goes on to explain one experience that involved Dad's loss of a buddy. "That's when he broke down when telling this story ... Even at my young age, I could tell he was proud of his uniform and very proud of his country." Thank you, Jerry, not only for remembering my dad in this manner but also for providing a reminder to us all that our children are listening, watching, and understanding their environment.

Because of the condition of the original citation, and because this is his original award, I have chosen to leave it as is. I have, however, retyped the original citation below, for your ease in reading. My dad was a most patriotic man.

Technician Fourth Grade Charles R. Dykens (Army Serial No. 37408216), United States Army. For gallantry in action during the initial landing operation in the invasion of France, 6 June 1944. In the landing of the strongly-held fortified enemy coast in the vicinity of Vier-ville-sur-Mer, France, Technician Fourth Grade Dykens, a vehicle driver, had the mission of driving ashore one piece of assault transportation, a responsibility that he successfully discharged under heavy enemy artillery and mortar fire.

Unable to get his vehicle off the beach because no exit had yet been cleared, Technician Fourth Grade Dykens, observed the evacuation of the wounded to the small boats and immediately began to drive along the beach under a constant hail of enemy fire and without regard to personal safety as he used his vehicle to collect and deliver numerous wounded to the assault craft which were waiting to evacuate them. This gallant example of courage and determination to be of service was an inspiration to his comrades on the beach and reflects great credit upon Technician Fourth Grade Dykens and upon the entire Military Service. Entered Military Service from Pierce City, Missouri.

SPANKINGS AND SUCH

Because we were located on a prairie, we had an outdoor classroom right at our back door. There was a time when I could have identified most of the grasses, plants, trees, birds, animals, insects, and flowers in that area. On one of these excursions, when I was in the second grade, I created my own field trip. The whole school had ventured out onto the prairie this particular day. Our teacher had us under control, and in theory, we were learning a bunch. About a half mile from the school, we had gathered and were having a lesson on what we were learning that day. As we finished and prepared to start back, I had an idea. I remember thinking how proud my teacher, Ms. Wommack, would be of what I was about to do. I talked one of the girls in my grade (sorry, I don't remember her name) into taking off with me and beating everyone else back to the school. It may have been Mary Kendrick or Janice Trenton; these were my fellow graduates in the eighth grade. But there very well may have been others in my second-grade class. Anyway, we took off running, and in spite of a loud warning from our teacher, we ran faster. I realized later that she dared not leave the others to chase us.

We arrived at the school well ahead of the others. I seated myself at the teacher's desk. I had the girl stand next to me. I had our second-grade reader in hand, and she was reading to me as I pretended to be the teacher. I just knew that when Ms. Wommack walked through that back door and saw the scene, she would be so proud. Why, I figured she would give us each a big gold star for our efforts and would surely brag on us in front of the whole school. I believe to this day that she was proud. I know I saw a glimpse of "Oh my goodness, would you just look at that beautiful little boy pretending to be me" on her face. It was right about here that my plan fell completely apart.

All I know for sure is that I spent the rest of the afternoon with my nose in a ring. This was a form of punishment applied for various offenses, and depending on the severity of the crime, the time an offender spent with his or her nose in the ring was anywhere from very short to very, very long. The ring had been drawn on blackboard, and there I stood for the rest of the day. At least I had committed my crime during an afternoon trip. And yes, she did tell my parents. And yes, I got in trouble at home too. For you parents who practice the philosophy of child rearing today, I commend you. As one who retired from the public school system, I urge you to support your schools and to stay in constant communication with the teachers and administration. Please don't assume you have heard the whole story as you listen to it around the dinner table. If you don't gather at the dinner table, I beg you to find time to do that. It really is a good place to get acquainted with your kids. Sorry; that's been instilled in me for a long, long time. Trust me; your kids will respect you for it. Most parents do a great job of staying in touch with the school and their kids, so please don't take offense at my venting. I'll share with you what my mom used to tell me when she would start lecturing her kids on various things: "If the shoe fits you, put it on." And that is all I have to say about that.

The above story is a hint, at least to some degree, of how discipline was handled in the one-room country school. It seems appropriate at this time to approach the subject of discipline with a little more insight into the expectations of elementary students attending Scotland Elementary School. In my tenure as a high school principal and classroom teacher, I was subjected to many different philosophies of discipline. Over time, I developed my own, because as it is with most things, change becomes necessary in our approach to solve problems. What was handed out to us in the form of discipline at Scotland would not, for the most part, be acceptable in classrooms of today. But it was sound, it fit those times, and it was handed out for the same reasons discipline today should be handed out. Very simply, I believe discipline should be handed out for the purpose of teaching self-discipline. That became my philosophy. As I progressed in my chosen profession, I soon learned that teaching one to use self-discipline was easier said than done. And rules were certainly necessary—especially rules that were needed and that, if followed, would result in positive results.

I really do not recall the employment of a long written list of rules in our one-room country school. I do remember we had discipline, and thus we had school. So we did have rules. They were simple and very measurable. I don't remember a long list of rules because we didn't have one. They were not listed in a student handbook; for that matter, they weren't even listed. If they were listed, I don't remember them being posted for our reading pleasure. I do remember the rules, just not a list. I may have forgotten a couple, but the hidden list we all knew went something like this:

Don't speak without permission.
Stay on task.
Don't bother your neighbor.
Stay in your row.
Don't touch the stove.
Share.
Show respect.
Don't wear hats inside.
Children in the fourth grade down need to have an upper-class
    escort to make a trip to the outhouse.

Help each other.
Stay out of the coal shed.
Don't climb the flagpole.

Other rules were added on as needed. There were many, and you get the idea. So what happened when we broke a rule? We didn't have a discipline grid as such. I can speak from experience, however, in stating that our teachers were very good at making the punishment fit the crime, so to speak. We only had to know that we were in trouble and that we would be held accountable both at school and at home. Once in a while we had the responsibility of delivering a note from the teacher explaining the incident. Oh yes, it got delivered because it would be a whole lot worse if it didn't and sooner or later the truth came out. It was a small community, and there were no secrets. Most of time, though, we were expected to simply tell our parents exactly what happened, leaving nothing out. That was hard to do but effective.

I used this method many times over the years as a principal. I would say, "You are to tell your parents exactly what has happened." They knew that if I didn't hear from their parents the very next day, if not that same day, I would be calling them. That meant additional consequences on top of what had already taken place. Most students did well with this, but of course, on several occasions, it was necessary we all get together and get our stories straight. That was good, because even if we didn't agree, we communicated. In my opinion, we need more of this in today's society than ever before. Okay, I am off on another part of my life. Sorry about that, but it was a lesson I learned in the one-room school and was able to apply to a fairly large high school of about eight hundred students.

Some of the more common applications of punishment at Scotland were as follows: Placing our nose in a ring drawn on the blackboard was used most often. The length of time we stood in that position was somewhat negotiable.

Note that the punishment of a child is a serious happening. While I would question the nose in the ring in today's environment, it was appropriate at this time in our history. I wish I could say that I was always right in what I did in my experiences as a principal. I tried to be, but many, many times I knew later that I should have handled a particular case differently. Even in the raising of my own sons, I sure would like to have some do-overs. I share this with you in the hope that you discipline for one reason only, and that is to help one to learn self-discipline. Even when you must discipline, you should do so with love. If you are reading this book, I know I am preaching to the choir.

Revocation of recess privileges wasn't used all that often, because our teacher, bless her heart, needed a break. However, it was employed on occasion.

Paddling did happen, but not very often. When it was applied, the discipline took place in the cloakroom and out of sight of the other students. Of course, we could all hear.

Being made to stay after school was a rarity, but it did happen. If an offense was serious enough, this punishment was administered. The teacher knew that the parents would soon get word of what had happened and that they would be there as soon as possible.

Cleaning the blackboard and erasers was used as punishment for some of the lesser infractions and was to be done on our time: during recess, before school, after school, during lunchtime, and so forth. Note: cleaning the erasers was also used as a reward, the difference being that we could do it on school time. Since we got to go outside to do this, we often volunteered for it.

Sending a note home requesting a conference with our parents was very effective. It was not a good thing to be given such a note.

Carrying in coal and water wasn't used as punishment very often. It actually was an assigned duty for the janitor, but on occasion, it did happen. I liked to get this as a punishment during my eighth-grade year because I was the janitor and had to do it anyway. Usually the janitor of the school was the teacher. Most of the time, it was a part of their contract.

These were all possibilities for punishment, but the truth is that ending a problem most often took only a stern look, a tap on the shoulder, a verbal warning, a private conversation, an apology, a handshake, or simply a promise (a contract) that it would not happen again. When our teacher was disappointed in us, it hurt.

This pretty much sums up my remembrance of rules and punishments. Yes, some of them were well defined, but in short, we were expected to behave appropriately. If we didn't, we were held accountable. The rules didn't have to be listed. The right and wrong ways to act were not that complicated. I will close this chapter with my testimony from twenty-nine years of being a high school principal. I never was as good as my elementary teachers were in successfully teaching students that all we really need to do is treat others as we wish to be treated. Somewhere along the line, it became much more complicated. I am not saying we didn't have discipline, because we certainly did. But I am saying it was a very different environment than I experienced in my one-room country schoolhouse.

CURRICULUM: THE THREE Rs PLUS SOME

You know what? We had a pretty fair offering that seemed to meet the needs of the time we lived in. There is no doubt life was much simpler then. Still, the challenge was to send us forth with at least a minimal mastery of knowledge. Just as happens today, some found this easier than others. Our teachers were pretty good at individualizing instruction. They took pride in the philosophy they were taught concerning the education of every child. They took every child as far as they could from where he or she was in the time they had, knowing that the children would all arrive at different levels. Many of you will recognize this as the central point of Bloom's Taxonomy. Have we lost that goal? I want to believe that we have not. But maybe we have slipped some.

At Scotland, our curriculum consisted of very basic courses designed for each grade level, with lots of hands-on and self-taught learning. This pretty much had to be the style, as we had only one teacher for all eight grades. The physical arrangement was that each row of desks would house a particular grade. Once in a great while, we would have more people in a row than the desks in one row could accommodate. When this happened, that class would simply spill over into the next row, filling up the back seats first.

Since the desks were on runners with three or four desks attached to one set of runners, this was our only option.

I know you are expecting me to tell you that our curriculum consisted entirely of reading, writing, and arithmetic. And with the exception of the agricultural science I had as an eighth grader, some science integrated into the math curriculum, and some conservation studies of both plants and animals, we had little exploratory science curriculum. I will say, though, that during my eighth-grade year we did purchase a science kit. Needless to say, we did lots of memorization (especially poems), Bible verses, and spelling words. Spelling was a daily test. We did not have practice tests. We practiced at home and took the test every day at school. The bad part of this was that we learned to spell pretty much by memorization. The drill was to write each word twenty-five times in preparation for each daily test. This isn't to say that phonics were not utilized; they were, but if all else failed, we would memorize. Be it a math rule, a poem, a Bible verse, or a spelling word, we would read it, write it, or spell it. Even to this day, I can usually tell when I misspell a word because it just doesn't look right.

We had reading groups, math groups, and even some science groups. These groups were organized not by grade level but by ability level. I really don't think we knew the difference. It was simply the group I went to for my lesson in a given subject. At least *I* didn't know the difference. That tells you what group I was in, doesn't it.

I have no idea how many books I read. I can tell you it was a bunch. In fact, it was in my early intermediate grades that I wrote some books. By the way, two of my grandchildren—Dixie when in sixth grade and Bode when in fourth grade—were writing stories and short books in school. Now as a sophomore and an eighth grader, they are still reading lots of books. My two younger grandchildren, Sevilla, age eight, and Eliana, age five, are reading up a storm too. Sevi has already begun to write some stories on her own, and Ellie will soon be doing that as well. It isn't just my grandchildren; I see lots of kids doing this. As a parent or grandparent, my advice is to encourage this activity and to accommodate it but don't push too hard. Let them explore. They will figure it out. I hope we never stop insisting that our kids read good books.

I suspect many children like these I mention are having this same experience. I hope so. It usually happens in the intermediate grades as far as wanting to write a book. Please allow me to explain a little further. When I first started writing, I called it "writing a book." What I was doing was writing a short story and calling it a book. I remember my teacher bragging on me and the more she bragged, the more I wrote. My favorite time, when I was in second grade or thereabouts, was story time. Every day, our teacher would read a story that all eight grades would listen to. I am not sure what grade level the stories were at, but I do know she made them interesting for everyone. We loved them! When I finally was promoted to the eighth grade, I was still enjoying those stories. I promised her that one day I would write a real book. This may not be it, but it is on my bucket list. I'll keep trying until I get it done.

The routine was for the teacher to start her teaching portion of the day and work her way across the room, grade by grade, one row at a time. The rest of us were working independently, in groups by grade level, in a teacher-organized group, or helping tutor others. I can still hear her hollering across the room to me, "Raymond, you lead that group, and be ready for the lesson when I get there." She might go on to add, "Have it done, and be ready to show me your work." Today we call this "cooperative learning." And yes, if done correctly, it works. And yes, we were ready when she got to our group. We were prepared with what we could accomplish on our own, and what we couldn't do she explained and walked us through it. She would either brag on us or share with us how disappointed she was that we had not tried harder to successfully complete the work on our own. She never put us down, though. She continually encouraged us to do better—not because we had to but because we could.

Grade cards went home quarterly. They reported not just our grades in math, science, reading, language arts, and spelling, but also our marks on citizenship, behavior, and participation. Moms and dads took all these grades seriously—especially the behavior grade. Learning was fun! We were on the blackboard a bunch, ciphering, spelling, having math contests, and even showing off our artistic skills. We competed in science projects and wrote poems, stories, books, and even songs. Competition was incorporated a lot, and we loved winning. But she also taught us not to be afraid of failure. She taught us that it was not a disgrace to fail. Instead it was an opportunity to improve and get better. We came to understand that the only person we had to beat was ourselves. An eighth-grade comprehensive examination given us by the county superintendent of schools, told the story of our opportunity to graduate from the eighth grade. Some had to take the examination more than once. All three of the graduates in my class had to take it only once!

The Pledge

Honoring America was an important part of our curriculum. Each day started, weather permitting, with the pledge being recited at the flagpole. If this was not possible, we did it immediately after the hand-washing routine, as we stood at attention by our assigned desks. Standing straight, tall, and proud, we put our right hands over our hearts and kept our eyes on the flag located to the right of the teacher's desk at the front of the room. This was the standard. It was the start of our curriculum each day and was probably one of the more important things we learned—at least in my opinion. One of us, each day, was chosen to lead the pledge. It was considered an honor, and every student in the school was honored in this way.

Our First Science Kit: Easy on the Combustion

I'll never forget the first science experiment kit ever owned by our little school. The money earned to purchase it came from an auction of pies, quilts, and crafts made by moms, dads, and kids. My contribution to that effort was a crocheted rug. It was made from women's old hose and pieces of cloth from old clothes, such as worn-out jeans and men's ties, and tied together. It was oval in shape and was indeed a rug of many colors. I don't remember who bought it or how much it brought. I just knew I made it. Anyway, we got our science kit. Until now, we had never seen chemicals, flasks, a Bunsen burner, or all sorts of directions on things we could make and what they meant. Even our teacher had to learn along with us on this one. Together we learned and were able to do some very simple but meaningful scientific experiments. We learned about gravity, osmosis, and combustion. (It did get a little smoky, but there was no real fire.) Perhaps the greatest lesson we garnered from our experiment was how to follow instructions. We finally had some real science going on.

I know it sounds bad to some that we didn't have much. My high school days were not much better. I did take a chemistry class during those days, and I will honestly tell you that we had only one Bunsen burner and very little equipment. And the rest of that story is that I went off to college and was enrolled in a five-hour botany course immediately. I was in some deep, deep *stuff*. But that is another story for another time.

Fine Arts Required

The fine arts were a very important part of our curriculum. We had many opportunities to sing, play a musical instrument, act, and recite in public performances. Shoot, we even had our own band, complete with a bazooka section, a sticks section, a tambourine section, and a couple of drums, and of course a piano and guitar would join in. It taught me to love music, and to this day I still enjoy strumming my guitar and singing a song. On one particular occasion, I was privileged to be a part of a family band. Our son Alan, about age twelve at the time, was on banjo; our son Andy, about age ten, was on fiddle; and our friends Mary, Glenn, and Verlene were on piano, guitar, and bass, respectively. We played and sang some country, bluegrass, and gospel. I know it all came from the one-room country school and the fun we had with music.

Our little band finally faded away because Glenn and I couldn't change chords fast enough to keep up, and hitting a minor chord was not in our résumés—at least not mine. Seriously, my wife and I count these times among our most treasured family experiences. Even today we all get together once in a great while and play some music. Gosh, I miss those times.

Bible Verses

Yes, Bible verses were a part of the curriculum. Following the pledge each morning, we learned a new Bible verse for the day. By the end of the week, we had memorized five. We were often called on to recite the previous day's verse, or perhaps all five we had learned for that week. Of course, the little ones couldn't get them all. But you would be surprised at how many they did remember. After all, we were all in the same room and quickly learned that little ears hear a bunch and can often repeat what they hear, whether it is good or bad. This is not a bad lesson for us to keep in mind today—wouldn't you agree? I do understand why we can't teach Bible verses in our public schools of today. But from my own selfish and research-based experience, I believe with all my heart that the day we kicked God out of our schools was the same day we slipped in our teaching of such values as honesty, integrity, respect, self-discipline, sharing, trust, and, obviously, faith. And I refer here not just to "a faith" but rather to the faith we need to have in ourselves and in others. Are these not values that transcend politics and religion? For our schools out there still teaching these kinds of values, I applaud you! For those that are not, please give it some thought. I believe we can separate the church and the state and yet agree on these very basic and necessary citizenship standards. Don't you?

Come and Get It: Teaching Fractions

Lunchtime was special in so many ways. It, too, was even special as a learning tool, and so I include a part of it under the writings about our curriculum. I always looked forward to lunch. I still do!

Our teacher made sure she lost no opportunities to learn from our everyday experiences. I remember she would call us up to her desk at lunchtime. We would go up one at a time, and she would offer to help us cut our sandwiches. At least that was the reason she gave us. Depending on our group or grade level in math, she would ask us if we wanted our sandwich cut into halves, quarters, fifths, sixths, and so on. Or she might ask if we wanted it cut into triangles, rectangles, or perhaps a combination of squares, triangles, and such. She would do oranges and apples the same way. Then, in exchange for providing the service, she would levy a small charge. Usually, the price was one small piece of the sandwich. Once in a while, she would say, "No charge." She then would gather up all the pieces she had been paid by those that had plenty, and she would go up and down each row, making sure every boy and girl had something to eat on that day.

It was not uncommon for someone to have forgotten his or her sandwich, or so he or she would say. Others maybe had a little something but not nearly enough. Many, like me, had plenty. No, we were not rich in material things, but we did have plenty to eat and clean clothes to wear. Now, if you think the moms of this community didn't know what was going on, think again. I am very confident my mom always packed a little extra, and I suspect others in the community did the same.

It was a beautiful sight, as I look back on it. I don't know how much extra our teacher brought from her own icebox, but it was a bunch, I'm sure. The point is that every boy and girl had something to eat for lunch every day. Yes, it was both a fun and learning experience to get to go up to the teacher's desk at lunchtime. Little did we know at the time how valuable the lesson she was teaching us was. Not only did we learn some fractions and some geometry, but we also learned about sharing, sticking together, helping others, caring, and compassion. I thank God for those special lessons, and I cherish the souls that taught them to me. I doubt seriously they learned these types of teaching techniques in their formal schooling.

What We Really Learned

Ours was a curriculum packed with what we needed at the time. Of course, it would not fit the needs of today's world. But many years later, I figured out that what I really learned wasn't just math, science, history, and how to read. What I really learned from that one-room country school that allowed me to grow in my chosen career was much more than that. I learned a work ethic, a love for learning, how to ask questions, and how to get along with other people. Folks, these are the real basics—not the three Rs, but self-discipline. This means knowing right from rong and then doing the right thing. There is a right and rong to every decision. Right? Yes, wrong is spelled "rong." The five Rs are readin', ritin', rithmetic, rite, and rong. Sacrifice is a key to really understanding the Golden Rule and doing your best. In simple terms, that means being all that you can be and treating others the same way you wish to be treated.

Sorry for the sermon, but I believe this, and I believe these were the treasures in the chest of tools given to me, as a graduation present, from Scotland Elementary School, my one-room country school.

CHAPTER 18

LUNCHTIME

I did mention lunchtime as a time for learning, but believe me—it was an adventure. Really, you would have had to experience it, and some of you have, to even begin to appreciate it. At Scotland Elementary School, it was first of all a shared experience—shared in more ways than one. And it was not only a time to eat; it was a time to play, visit, rest, dream, gossip, and even study if you so desired. I'll begin with our hot lunch program.

Chili Day (Served Burnt)

Chili day was a special day that occurred maybe six or seven times a year. I guess you could say it was our attempt to initiate a hot lunch program. Each student, except for a few designated to bring crackers, brought a can of beans, and the teacher would bring the chili. We would add the ingredients and start it cooking in a big pot on the coal stove. This was the same stove that provided the heat for the entire room, and so it was going pretty strong. By at least noon, it would be ready to eat. We always enjoyed these steamy hot lunches of chili and crackers. Now, this sounds pretty good, doesn't it? "Not always" is my answer. On more than one occasion, we burned the chili. It is pretty hard to regulate a coal stove. Stirring helped, but still it was a pretty iffy deal.

On one of these burnt chili days, I and a couple of girls (our whole eighth-grade class) were allowed to walk home and get some bread, peanut butter, and whatever our moms had lying around and bring it back to the school. It was the only option for the kids to have something to eat. Usually we were able to eat burnt chili, but on this day it was really, really burnt. Janice, Mary, and I, all big-shot eighth graders, were given this assignment. Although we were to hurry, we were cautioned to be careful on our journey to get to our homes. To get there we had to cross a bridge that was a part of a very busy highway. I speak of Route 166. I've already mentioned this was a spur of the famous Route 66. The bridge was built over a creek that often was dry. I decided, after we were out of earshot of our teacher, that in order to get back as soon as possible, we could cut across the prairie and wade the creek. That's right; the creek was running full on this particular day.

Until we arrived at the creek, I really was feeling quite proud of myself for coming up with this idea. The creek was flowing fairly fast, and I immediately saw that this was not going to be easy. However, I was in charge, and I decided we could do it, and so across we started, wading, stepping on rocks, and trying our best to not fall in. Of course, we all fell in, and by the time we got home soaking wet, explained our plight, and headed back, we had lost a bunch of time. The school did get fed, and needless to say, I was in big trouble. You would have thought I should have learned my lesson from that first field trip I took on my own—yes, the one I told you about that happened when I was in the second grade. I was in trouble with the teacher for not sticking to the route we had agreed on before we left the school, with my parents for not obeying the teacher, and with my classmates and their parents. To this day, I don't believe the chili was burned too badly to eat to begin with. Regardless, I learned an important lesson for life. I really did learn this time; I promise. Sticking to a plan isn't all that bad of an idea. I'll not go into what the punishment was at school and at home. For sure, the fine fit the crime.

Trading Lunches

Weather permitting, we were allowed to take our lunches outside. This became our trading market. If I had a Sno Ball cake and I wanted a Baby Ruth candy bar, I had a decent chance. If I had a potted meat sandwich and wanted anything else, I had no chance. Some liked apples, some oranges, and some bananas. And so these were good trading items. A banana and a peanut butter and jelly sandwich could get you two Sno Ball cakes and a stick of licorice candy—that is, if you played your cards right.

Of course our teacher was aware of these trades. I remember her assigning the seventh- and eighth-grade students the job of being sure the little ones didn't get cheated in the process. Most of the time, the first and second graders had to eat in the presence of the teacher, and so it usually was not a problem. I do remember, though, having to look after my brother. He liked Sno Ball cakes a lot. Once in a while I would even get really brave and trade my whole sack and its contents. There were no questions asked and no hints given. It was, shall we say, a gamble. My experience in this risky trade was that I could not always tell the contents of a sack by its size or weight. It was just a bet. I once traded for some rocks and a few crackers. Don't feel bad for me. In my sack I traded away were some walnuts and a hammer to crack them with. Okay, okay, I'm not being completely honest about the rocks. But I am honest when I say that we were pretty good at disguising what we had in our sacks. Was it a hammer and walnuts or was it a big peanut butter and jelly sandwich, a banana, and a couple of Sno Ball cakes? I leave the truth of this story's end to you.

Washing Hands

This was not only a standard at lunchtime; it was a ritual several times a day. When school opened, we lined up and washed our hands. Our teacher knew that we had played all the way to school and there would be no telling what we may have explored with our hands. We lined up again after each recess. And we lined up again whenever the teacher felt that we needed to, which was fairly often. Of course, many of us visited the ole washbasin on an individual and as-needed basis. Needless to say, trips to the outhouse were not negotiable.

The older kids all had jobs. Water had to be carried in from the outside pump. The water had to be rationed and poured over the hands. It was hard to keep track of whose turn it was at the water and soap stations. Following that, we headed to the rinse station and then on to a paper towel station. Paper towels had to be handed out, so as not to be wasteful, and all of the above had to be cleaned up after each experience. We often would sing songs during these washing rituals. Pouring the water was the best job, and so we had to take turns at that one. Yep, we learned to take turns and to accept responsibility, and to quote my mother, we were often reminded that "cleanliness is next to godliness."

Speaking of cleanliness, I need to share with you another one of my embarrassing stories. In fact, I am remembering other stories that don't really fit into a nice, thematic chapter title. But they are representative of my time at Scotland Elementary School and are precious recollections of what I did—and in some cases should not have done. Enjoy!

OTHER STORIES THAT COME TO MIND

Tongue on the Pump Handle

I know you have all heard stories of little kids being dared to place their tongues on a frozen pump handle or flagpole (as Ralphie did in the movie *A Christmas Story*). Yes, I was one of those kids. And I am ashamed to admit that I was not a little kid and no one dared me to do it, and yes, I did know better. At least I should have. It happened on a freezing winter day when I was sent to carry in another bucket of water in preparation for the washing of hands before lunch. I must have been at least a seventh grader. As I was pumping the water with gloves on my hands, I got to thinking. Oops! That has always been a dangerous thing for me to do. Anyway, I began trying to figure out how it could be that one's tongue could stick to a frozen pump handle. It made no sense to me. I knew my breath was warm, my mouth was moist, and after all, it wasn't as if the handle was ice coated. I convinced myself the whole thing was a story that had been made up to scare little kids. So I just had to prove them wrong. Yep, I did it! I stuck the tip of my tongue on the pump handle. If I had touched it in the place where I had placed my hands, which were covered with gloves, I might have been all right. But no, I had to prove my theory without any variables. Yes, literally, I was stuck. There I stood, by myself, embarrassed, mad, and somewhat scared.

At this point, I was determined to free myself before someone came looking for me. My plan was for no one to ever find out about this happening. Slowly, I tried pulling away from the pump handle. No luck! Then I noticed the bucket of water I had filled. It was sitting right by my feet. By pushing the pump handle down, I could reach it. I remember trying to figure it out. I came to the conclusion that since the water in the bucket was not frozen, it surely must be warmer than the pump handle. I've already told you I was in the seventh grade and that we had a new science kit in our school.

I reached down, got a handful, of water and splashed it on both the pump handle and my mouth. Then I gave a slight pull back. It hurt! I was still stuck! So I repeated the process at least three or four more times. I hoped it would work, because if not, I was adding more ice to the already frozen pump handle. Now, please remember that we did not have a TV and that *A Christmas Story* was not in my memory bank at this point. Nor should it have been, since it wasn't released until 1983. But if I would have had that scene implanted in my mind, as many of you do, I would not have been in that position. Until now, I have not shared this true story with anyone. I even believe this will be my family's first reading. Since the incident, I have seen *A Christmas Story* several times, and I love that scene. It is so real to me.

Yes, I did free myself. To the best of my knowledge, no one knew of this happening. Yes, my hypothesis was wrong. It isn't a made-up story intended to scare little kids. And yes, I did peel a bit of skin off the tip of my tongue. But by keeping my mouth shut for the rest of the day, I was able to conceal it. Come to think of it, keeping my mouth shut perhaps would solve lots of problems and would be a good secondary lesson to this story. Remember, kids: it is not a scare tactic. It is true!

The pump pictured in the front cover of this book is a replica of the one that did damage to my tongue and my pride. You can see its relation to the school and what was going through my mind regarding someone coming to look for me. The pump pictured is one I found on some recently purchased property in Lamoni, Iowa. It still works and will serve as a backyard "water the flowers" pump. It, like me, is showing its age, but it has so many stories stored within its history that I just can't part with it. Each of its rust spots and scars has a story behind it. I, of course, will never know its full history, but it reminds me of the same one I had a personal acquaintance with at Scotland Elementary School. It makes me smile, and at my age, smiling is a wonderful way to start the day.

The Window Blinds (The Truth behind Them)

I have mentioned the bay of windows on the east side of our schoolroom several times in this book. They ran nearly the entire length of that side of the room. They were equipped with pull-down shades, and often they were in the pulled-down position in the morning to keep the sun out. As they were on the east side, it was just too bright on sunny days. So why do they deserve their own little space in my book? I, too, am wondering that as I type this little story. But again, it is a true story, and I feel compelled to mention it. Let me just say that they were a great place to crawl behind. The window ledge was wide; one could not see through the blinds, and so it was a good place to have some degree of privacy. Privacy from what, you ask?

I need to be perfectly clear right here and now of my lack of experience with what went on behind those blinds. In fact, in my early grades especially, I was the president of the local "women haters' club." And in my later grades—sixth, seventh, and eighth—while I did drop out of the club, I was still, shall we say, not very social around the girls. The same can't be said for some of my classmates. These blinds became a hideout for certain boys and girls to steal a kiss. Yep, that's right! Like you, I couldn't believe it, and I thought it so disgusting that I once reported it to the teacher. I thought it was my civic duty. Yep, I told on them. All she said to me was "One day you'll understand. Don't worry about it; I have my eye on them."

She, of course, was right. I am truthful when I tell you that I never did take advantage of these "blind dates." But I will say it did spawn my interest some, and so, as predicted by my teacher, I did fall in love with a beautiful girl, and now I understand. After fifty-four years of marriage, my wife, Glenna Jean Allison Dykens, still puts up with me. If she had been in Scotland Elementary School with me, I honestly believe I would have felt differently about those blinds.

Head Janitor (The Bike Shall Be Mine)

I truly can say that we did have a janitor for our little school, at least for my eighth-grade year. It was yours truly. I really don't think this was the standard. I remember dads doing it, the teacher doing it, and moms doing it. It could be that because my dad was on the board, I got the job. But more than likely, it was because he paid me out of his own pocket and was responsible for seeing that it got done. I am not sure, but I do know it was turned over to me and I did it.

There were times, of course, when I needed a little help. But for the most part, I took care of it. I took this opportunity very seriously. My dad trained me, monitored me, and made sure I was skilled in what I had to do. I really didn't know what I was getting into, but I was determined to not fail. My day would start early in the morning, and as I recall, that would be about thirty minutes prior to the arrival of the teacher. That would be about an hour before the students were scheduled to arrive. Most of the time, my dad was able to take me on his way to work in Joplin, Missouri. But on the days when he couldn't do that, I had to walk. I was age thirteen and had my own key to the school. My dad even made me a key ring with my name on it. I still have it.

So, about seven in the morning, I would open up the school. If necessary, my first job was to get the fire going. It usually was not a problem because I had banked it the night before. My next job was to carry in two buckets of water to start the day with. One was for washing, and the other for drinking. I opened the blinds to let in the light, carried in more coal to support the ongoing fire, put paper towels in place, placed toilet paper near the back door, and, if needed, shoveled or at least swept the steps. I had to monitor the toilet paper as the day went on. Students would pick it up at the back door when they went to the outhouse and return it when they came back—sometimes, that is. I cleaned the blackboard if necessary. Most of the time, it had been done the night before. Dusting was not my favorite thing to do, but it was an important morning chore. The piano, teacher's desk, library table, bookshelves, and, especially, the teacher's chair all had to be dusted. As part of the early-morning readiness by students, they all had to dust their own desks.

The last thing I did before the students began to arrive was raise the flag. Sometimes we would have a flag-raising ceremony, but most of the time it was my responsibility to appropriately raise it. I did this on my own until, at my dad's suggestion, I got an assistant. There is a proper way to raise the flag. One thing is for sure; it must never touch the ground. I learned from my dad, a WWII Veteran, that the proper way to raise our flag is to raise it "briskly." When lowering the flag, it should come down slowly and with respect. It always bothered my dad over the years when someone would raise or lower the flag inappropriately. This would often happen at high school events when students raised it in time with the play-ing of the national anthem. Just take note, and you will see this happening all the time. Flag etiquette says to raise it "briskly, proudly, and with a steadiness." Anyway, to be sure this all happened, I found a helper. Whoever it was had to hear the same training I had received from my dad. I loved, and still love, raising the flag.

During the day, my janitorial chores were limited, but occasionally the teacher would call on me for more coal or water, or perhaps to escort a young man to the outhouse and back. Of an evening, I often had help from Mom or Dad or both—but not always. We swept the floor every day with a chemically treated sawdust. We sprinkled it on the floor, and when we swept it up, it did a great job of collecting all the dirt and even the dust. The hard part was moving the rows of desks so we could sweep under them. But with a little help, we could slide the runners sideways until we could clean the area vacated by them. We did each row in this manner, and lastly we would go back and sweep all the aisles. After the sweeping was done, I banked the coal stove, shut the draft, locked all doors, and emptied the water buckets and cleaned them for use the next morning.

I told you it was a job. And it was. I was a paid employee. My pay was ten dollars a month for eight months—eighty dollars for the school year. We went to school for only eight months each year. If you are not of a generation that went for only eight months, you may be asking, "Why?" There were probably more reasons than I will explain, but mainly it was because of the agrarian culture of that time. Actually, it was coming to an end, and many of the larger schools were beginning to add time to their school calendars. But the one-room school was truly in the country. Many students lived on farms, and frankly they were needed at home during the planting season and also to keep up with the many chores associated with the farming community. Money, too, was probably a factor. Hiring a teacher for another month, keeping the building open for another month, and losing help at home for another month were all monetary factors affected by a nine-month school year. But, of course, times did change, and finally more and more schooling was necessary. Surely most of you will remember that getting a high school diploma was the ultimate goal.

Anyway, I figure that because we didn't have kindergarten, and because for eight years I went for only eight months a year, I got shorted out of two years of formal schooling. I lost not only a month of learning each year but also another month's salary. Anyway, I honestly did save every penny I earned that year. With that money, I bought an English racer bicycle. The cost of the bike was seventy-nine dollars. That is the truth. You probably know the type I am talking about. It had seven or eight forward gears; very narrow tires; a small banana seat; narrow, streamlined handle bars; and it was shiny black with chrome trim. Since I lived in the country, this was not a very practical bike for me. The only paved road in the area was a very dangerous highway. But my parents couldn't talk me out of it, and so they let me learn a valuable lesson—and a costly one at that. You've probably already guessed the outcome. It was a great bike but was not the one I should have spent my hard-earned money on. Regardless, I rode it, and needless to say, I wore it out quickly. At least it was mine and I had earned it. In spite of the rocks and abuse, that bike and I covered the ground and had a great time together.

Community Involvement

Please understand that our community and our parents valued education, and even though for some lessons we were not formally in the schoolhouse, the community did make sure we had learning opportunities. I include the following pictures as examples of the involvement of our Scotland community in the lives of the children enrolled in Scotland Elementary School. You have read my mentions of car pools, pie suppers, programs, repair and replacement of playground equipment, transportation for field trips, upkeep of the grounds and buildings, entertainment, subbing for the teacher, and the like. But it went well beyond that.

I point out several times in this book that the community of Scotland was a community of involvement with their school. My brothers, along with classmates, learned by working under Mr. Snyder. I still have a Ping-Pong table I made in the eighth grade. You might say it was our shop class.

Woodworking is the choice of a project in the Echo Acres 4-H club. The members learn to mark and saw boards square in their beginning work. Four-H'ers in the more advanced years learn to make lawn chairs, table tennis tables and other pieces of furniture. In the picture above, Glen Snyder is demonstrating the proper method of marking and sawing a board. Echo Acres 4-H'ers in the picture are from left to right: Jerry Gaddis, Raymond Dykens, Frank Samson, John Gaddis, Ronnie Endicott, Mr. Snyder, Jerry Endicott, Jimmy Dykens and Bobby Dykens. Standing in front from left to right are: Chase Long and Freddie Endicott.

Echo Acres A Community Minded 4-H Club

P1

Garden projects provide 4-H'ers the opportunity to watch and study their garden grow. 4-H'ers pictured above harvesting one of the garden are, from left to right, Ronnie Endicott, Jerry Endicott and Bob Christman. The gardeners enjoy a tour of the members' gardens each year.

Graduates Mary, Ray, Janice

8th Grade Field Trip - Jefferson City, Mo. 1957

So many times this community gave time and money they couldn't afford to give. As I progressed in my career, I learned from some very good administrators that "if you are not doing it for kids, perhaps you should not be doing it." This community and its school was all about doing all they could do for kids. I offer these few pictures as testimony, and there are many names you will perhaps recognize. But others, too, not mentioned or pictured, were there for us as they maintained their school and community with the utmost integrity, respect, and pride. I am proud to have been a part of this happening.

The Three-Legged Rooster

Indulge me, if you will, in one more community story. To tell it, I must humble myself. Perhaps not as much as *the "tongue on the pump handle" story*, but still, I must say, it is a humbling story. This story is about a primary student who lived in Scotland, Missouri, and attended Scotland Elementary School. He was probably about old enough to begin first grade at Scotland Elementary School. He is guessing about this because he is hoping he was younger, as he should have known better. Anyway, he had a rooster that he fed and watered every day. At night, the rooster would leave and go someplace else to sleep. Morning would arrive, and he would come for his breakfast. This little boy decided he needed to figure out where this rooster was sleeping. One evening, long before dark, the rooster was already gone for the evening. This was the boy's chance to find out where Old Cock-A-Doodle Do had been going. He at least was smart enough to tell his parents what he was up to and ask them if they could help. His dad—a dad who loved to tease, I might add—told the boy that all he had to do was ask the neighbors if they had seen his three-legged rooster. He was sure the lad would get someone to remember seeing a three-legged rooster. So off he went.

I can tell you firsthand that no one admitted to seeing a three-legged rooster. The boy's uncle Walt and aunt Corella lived only a block away, and they were at least sympathetic with his concern for finding his three-legged rooster. The boy appreciated that because the only other help he had received was knowing that he had made some people laugh. And that was okay because his folks had taught him that a good belly laugh once in a while was good for the soul.

Anyway, his aunt promised him she would be on the lookout and help if she could. It wasn't long after this happening that she brought us over this picture. Did I tell you my uncle was a photographer? Anyway, there it was, sitting high on the hog—literally. They had found that it had been coming over every night and roosting on the back of their prize hog. This young lad was thankful for their help, for a couple of reasons. First, he had found the rooster and solved the puzzle. Secondly, he had learned how many legs a rooster has, and he figured that would be good information before he entered the first grade.

Yes, the story is true, and yes, it is about me. And yes, I am just as gullible today, but at least I get on the internet and research some before I set out to give a bunch of people a good belly laugh. I would say my rooster was pretty smart; wouldn't you?

CHAPTER 20

LEARNING THEN AND LEARNING NOW: MY THOUGHTS

As a retired educator, I am aware of the changes that have taken place over this past century relative to the process of learning. Certainly we are much better informed and much more aware now than we were at Scotland as to the mechanics of learning. The following are some of my thoughts and my interpretation of the labels we attached to what we were doing at the time. I offer it not as a comparison of which were right or wrong but merely as a conversation piece that suggests, at least to some degree, we had things moving in the right direction in our little one-room country schools. I hope you can agree that our students today are blessed with many, many more opportunities to learn. However, the basis of all learning is still pretty much the same. Learning is, even today, a work in progress. And so the basis of what should have been in the one-room country school and what should be in our school today is left for the last sentence of this chapter.

I'll begin with a philosophy shared with me by Dr. James Chrisman, superintendent of schools at Galena Public Schools in Galena, Kansas. He hired me as a high school principal, and I was honored and challenged to take his place in the superintendent's chair after his retirement. He taught me that whatever administrators do in this school system, we do it for kids. If we are not doing it for kids, we shouldn't be doing it. I clung to that philosophy and tried my best to continue its impact on the kids at Galena. It just makes sense, and it makes decision-making so much easier. No politics, no guessing, and no other choices would stand the test against what is best for kids. My point in telling you this is that, in my little school at Scotland, I honestly believe the community did exactly that. They didn't spell it out, but they made sure they were doing the best they could for the students in their school. And from my own experiences in my forty years as public educator and an employee of several different schools, I can honestly say, with few exceptions, that all of them tried as best they could to do what they did for kids. Of course, disagreements came up as to affordability and priorities of where we spent our money. It was a challenge at Scotland and remains a challenge even today as we try to keep up with the growth of technology and new fields of learning. If you are reading this, the bottom line will help in deciding. If you are not doing it for kids, don't do it.

New labels in today's school systems have had and continue to have an effect on our learning, and yet we move beyond those labels and get it done. For example, at Scotland Elementary School, we had group learning without a teacher actually being in the group all the time. We called it "get in your group, and be ready to explain to the teacher when she arrives." (Remember: eight grades being in one room was the challenge.) Today we call it cooperative learning and peer tutoring. Another important lesson we have learned in the business of educating our kids is that we should arrange time to promote learning. Unfortunately, for many years we arranged learning to facilitate time. At Scotland, we pretty much fell into the trap of yielding to the importance of time, and we built our learning around the clock. With eight grades in one room, there wasn't a lot of choice.

Only recently in our schools have we realized the importance of arranging time to fit learning. I am proud to say I was a pioneer in this movement. I learned of a system called block scheduling from the only school in the state of Missouri to implement it and immediately sold it to Carl Junction, Missouri—the school system I was in—and finally to the school I retired from in Galena, Kansas. It is a whole book in itself, but in short it allowed us to arrange time to facilitate learning.

The development of technology is, as many of you know, overwhelming. It has, of course, changed our entire methodology of learning. I believe it to be a tool that we must utilize, but I also believe it can never replace the human brain. I remain convinced that the best computer on the market is the human brain and that it is the development of the brain that we must continue to focus on. It was true at Scotland, and it's true now, in my opinion. Learn to use your brain; be able to make good choices by calling on the dents in your brain.

Anyway, as long as my grandchildren are near me, they can fix my smartphone and my computer, and they can even teach me about some of this stuff that is foreign to me. As the song goes, and it is one of my favorites, "Thank God for kids."

Discipline at Scotland and at Galena was, of course, not the same. Our discipline at Scotland was simple: swats, being made to stand with one's nose in the ring, and notes home. We never had a discipline grid. Today we have long ones. They spell out every consequence and what will happen if punishment is applied. I'll not go into all that, but I do know that if learning is to happen, you must have a disciplined environment in which to teach it. I stop there, as the pages to my book are limited.

Religion in our schools has been and continues to be a hot topic. I am of the belief that we can teach values like honesty, integrity, cleanliness, politeness, manners, free speech, loyalty, patriotism, self-discipline, and work ethic without crossing over the line that separates church from state. These are only a few of the values most of us cherish, and I hope you agree that they transcend both religion and politics. Yes, at Scotland, we did use religion as a tool to help us learn these values. Today we can't use religion as a tool in the school, but we can teach these same values because they transcend religion and politics. I'll leave it at that. I will close, though, by saying that there is no way to keep God out of the classroom if He is in your heart. That is your choice and not a choice of the state.

One thing I am very proud of in these United States is that from the very beginning we have set our goal to educate the masses. I am not saying we didn't have some learning to do in order to accomplish this goal. By "masses" I mean everyone: men, women, and all children, regardless of race, religion, sex, economic status, or political agenda. We still are working on getting it done. We are not there yet! But compared to the rest of the world, we are at least moving in that direction better than most. We must find a way to get it done! I could go on and on, but I promised you earlier that I would wind this chapter up with one last sentence that sums it up, in my opinion. If you are a student or a parent of a student, then I say to you that you are in a good learning situation and frame of mind if you understand and are being taught that learning is a lifelong process that requires you to learn from failure, to learn by application, to work hard, to do your best, and to have fun. Then and only then will you be able to go as far as you are capable of going in the act of putting dents in your brain for the rest of your life. I never said it would be easy. But I am saying this trip you are on is worth every bit of the experiences you will have on the journey. So says this old paw paw, and that is the *truth*.

Printed in the United States
By Bookmasters